Practical
Techniques
of Psychic
Self–
Defense

Practical Techniques of Psychic Self-Defense

by Murry Hope

St. Martin's Press
New York

Library of Congress Cataloging in Publication Data

Hope, Murry.
    Practical techniques of psychic self-defense.

    1. Occult sciences—Miscellanea.   I. Title.
II. Title: Psychic self-defense.
BF1439.H67   1986   133   85-26061
ISBN 0-312-63552-4 (pbk.)

First published in Great Britain by The Aquarian Press, Thorsons
Publishing Group.

10   9   8   7   6   5   4

CONTENTS

CHAPTER ONE

THE DEVELOPMENT OF PSYCHIC GIFTS

How many of us would think of rushing across a busy street without first checking for oncoming traffic or other obstacles? Few, no doubt, in their right mind would act so rashly. And yet otherwise sane and stable people will happily plunge headlong into unknown dimensions or uncharted areas of consciousness without observing even the simplest precautions. Which naturally gives rise to the question, 'What is there to be afraid of and why should we need to protect ourselves?' Fair comment. But before we take a look at the pitfalls of the psychic and occult path it is necessary to define our terms of reference.

Psychic, mystic, occultist: terms so often believed by the uninitiated to mean the same thing when this is not at all the case. The word 'psychic' is loosely used to cover a whole range of subjects such as psychometry, astral projection, ESP, the tarot, palmistry, and so on, but strictly speaking it relates to matters pertaining to the 'soul' or 'psyche', or to levels of comprehension that are not bounded by material dimensions.

In metaphysical parlance the psychic or mediumistic person is telepathically receptive, which means that he or she has the ability to tune in to other minds, incarnate or discarnate, or intelligences external to themselves and their own immediate environment. Genuine psychics are also able to tap that collective unconscious which exists interdependently of time and space; hence their ability to 'see' the past and future.

The word 'occult' simply means 'hidden' and is not synonymous with those dark practices that run against the tide of cosmic law, much as some of our Sunday newspapers would have us believe otherwise! The true occultist or magician is a person who aims to manipulate cosmic forces or subtler energies by using mind or will power, which skill is slowly (and sometimes painfully) mastered via a series of disciplines known as 'initiations'. An occultist may not be at all psychic, as was the case with the famous Elizabethan magus, Dr John Dee, who relied exclusively on the services of mediums. The occultist represents the positive or directive aspect of the metaphysical polarity, while the psychic or medium is on the negative/receptive side, the yang and yin as it were.

So what about the mystic? A mystic is a person, often of religious leanings, who takes his or her faith a step or more beyond the accepted dogmas of organized faiths and reaches out into the cosmos. In this searching he may neither direct cosmic energies nor receive their influences, but simply observe them.

During this observationary process the mystic enriches his soul with knowledge and understanding, without necessarily utilizing that knowledge in the practice of psychism or occultism. In fact, he may be totally unable to translate what he witnesses or feels, perhaps he does not have the necessary terms of reference to so do, but his experiences enable him to retain an air of sanctity and detachment from the normal *mêlée* of life.

Many mystics, however, are also psychics, healers or social workers, but they manage to exude a certain aura or charisma that hints at their having one foot in some other, perhaps more exalted, dimension.

There are those who function at the extreme end of the occult polarity, being either very positive/directive, and therefore needing a medium to polarize with in order to obtain the best results from their magical work, or negative/receptive, working best with an occultist or 'positive'. But there are also those who swing towards the centre and can adapt either way. A good working polarity of positive/negative will produce the best results, as the ancient cults and civilizations realized. Polarities such as priest/prophet, magus/scryer, pythoness/interpreter, and so on, as referred to in the historical records of many religions and traditions, will confirm the efficacy of the polarity system, which my own experience has also borne out.

Cosmic Law

Having established our terms of reference, we can now proceed to the question of the existence of cosmic law. The universe is not a haphazard chaotic conglomeration of life cycles. It follows an ordered pattern which accords with natural laws and is re-echoed in science, psychology and everyday existence. The apparent cycle of birth and death is consistent in all dimensions, as though the universe were constantly breathing in and out, each breath chalking up one more experience or area of knowledge to make up the whole.

When life forces flow with the forward directional impulses of cosmic law the results are harmonious, but when any mind or intelligence elects to travel along an opposing path somebody along that route suffers. Which brings us to the subject of evil.

Evil

There are many people who do not accept the existence of evil as a force or entity, implying that it is simply negative thinking which can be easily counteracted by ignoring its existence and thinking nice thoughts. All very pleasant if the other fellow follows the same line of logic and avoids stirring the mud but, unfortunately, if we are to face facts, the planet upon which we dwell is not all honey and brotherly love, and the thought-force generated by hatred alone produces enough unstable energy to cause untold suffering in the lives of many.

Universal or cosmic energy is a totally impersonal force, being neither good nor evil in itself. It only becomes 'black' or 'white', to use two rather crude and inflammatory terms, according to the intentions of the manipulator. And so it is in everyday life: we may use a fire to warm ourselves, heat our water, make ourselves more comfortable in chillier climes; or we can manufacture bombs which ignite the flames of human suffering!

People who try to effect advantageous social changes inevitably come up against those very regimes which have benefited from the previous order. This is also true in the psychic and occult worlds. I recall attending a trance address in London some years ago after which a couple in the audience asked the chairman why he was placing a protection around the medium. 'To ensure that the communicating entity is on the path of light, and not of evil intent,' he replied.

The couple, middle aged to elderly, seemed annoyed at this answer, declaring that they had been 'in that line of business' for some twenty-five years and had never encountered anything 'evil'. To which the able chairman replied, 'Well, madam, you have obviously never disturbed it!' the implication being that they had done little to enrich the lives of those around them, in spite of their frequent psychic encounters.

What is therefore generally termed 'evil' is actually misplaced or misdirected energy operating against the forward directional impulses of cosmic law, and evil people are simply those who misuse or misdirect natural forces, sometimes deliberately, sometimes through ignorance, to cause pain, suffering, destruction and chaos in any degree.

The subject of evil is a deep one and worthy of more consideration and debate than could be covered in a limited publication, but suffice it to say that subtle energies can be generated for selfish or destructive purposes, and what constitutes evil in one time zone or period of history does not necessarily do so in another. So in one sense ethics are relative to prevailing conditions in any area of human experience, whereas cosmic laws are constant, and it is upon this premise that we shall base our protective codes for the many fields of psychic and occult activity. Defining what is cosmically right and what is cosmically wrong can be summed up quite simply: evil is selfish and destructive, good is selfless and constructive.

Psychic Awareness

When a person starts to take an active interest in matters psychic or occult, certain transformations begin to take place in both his physical brain and psychological make-up. Scientists are still arguing about the role played by the physical brain but the general consensus of opinion is that the left hemisphere governs the normal logical processes of everyday living, encompassing such studies as mathematics, physics, technology and all practical or down-to-earth things; and the right hemisphere is more concerned with imagery, philosophy, religion, creative imagination and abstract concepts. A balanced and well-integrated personality will use both hemispheres to a certain degree, although in the western world the system of education does tend to over-emphasize left-hemisphere activity at the expense of the more mystical right side. This results in a rather materialistic society where TV and consumer goods rule rather than the finer and more sensitive human qualities.

With the advent of the Aquarian Age the swing the other way slowly commenced, as is so often the case after a period of spiritual repression, resulting in a sort of Open Sesame to anything metaphysical, no matter how way-out in some cases. So the right area of the brain suddenly becomes activated although the psyche has not yet coped with the programming necessary to keep the *persona* in balance. This will tend to produce groups of 'drop-outs', psychic degenerates, idiosyncratic and eccentric cults, plus a heavy toll of mental illness for the medical profession to clean up.

Any form of psychic development effects an expansion of consciousness, so that the rational thinking processes are required to take in a consideration of other dimensions or frequencies of existence beyond the ordinary day-to-day material world. In most cases the brain is able to compute the information fed to it from subconscious sources, decoding abstract concepts via symbology into terms of reference easily assimilated by the normal rationale and avoiding exaggerated fears or complete mental breakdowns. Only when this programming is not effective do the symptoms of mental illness commence to manifest, which naturally brings us to the question: is the psychic or occult path right for everyone?

As we are considering psychic self-defence perhaps I should rephrase that question: is it safe for everyone to 'dabble'? Or, assuming they intend to take a serious interest in the subject, is everyone suited to pursue the path of occultism, psychism or mysticism? To be absolutely honest the answer must be NO; just as not everyone can be a ballet dancer, doctor, bricklayer or explorer. The would-be psychic should first of all do some soul-searching and ask himself whether he is temperamentally suited to embark upon the exploration of his own inner consciousness and the greater universal unconscious.

It takes a strong and very stable personality to cope efficiently when exposed to conditions outside the programmed 'norm', as wiser folk than myself have explained in many previous publications; those who find themselves with natural psychic gifts should take great care that they observe the highway code of the cosmos, or they could find themselves tuning in to minds, or channelling energies, which are not always well intentioned or harmonious. Over the centuries the wise ones and incarnate 'old souls' have devised many systems for psychic and occult self-protection, which is what this book is all about.

Recognitions
Assuming that one is ready to proceed with psychic or occult development, one of the first things to do is to familiarize oneself with the sort of thing one is likely to encounter during excursions into uncharted areas of consciousness. The universe beyond the normal awareness of the five senses has been well mapped and sign-posted by those who travelled it before us and it is simply a question of learning how to read those signs.

There is a dictionary of archetypal symbology which always follows true. The subconscious mind, that part of the psychic economy which reaches out beyond time and space, communicates to its conscious counterpart via a form of cosmic shorthand or imagery. This language of the inner mind is by no means the exclusive territory of the occultist; psychiatrists, psycho-analysts and psychotherapists have plumbed its depths with effective skill over the past few years. It can be conveyed verbally as through a trance medium or clairvoyant, or via the many 'aids' or 'time-keys', to use the term I prefer to employ, such as the tarot, *I Ching*, runes, astrology, and so on. A detailed knowledge of archetypal symbology will soon show whether the aspiring psychic is:

1. Simply telepathizing with someone present
2. Genuinely travelling backward or forward in time
3. Indulging in an over-active imagination or wishful thinking
4. Mentally sick
5. A money-grabbing charlatan

It is always well to remember that the mind can be stretched sideways, as it were, and not necessarily always 'up' or 'down'. This is a mistake so often made by earnest meditators who are convinced that sitting cross-legged and thinking 'god' automatically links them into a hot line to heaven. More often than not they end up facing aspects of their own subconscious, 'id' or *alter ego*. But herein also lies a trap.

There is a school of thought currently popular, particularly amongst avid meditators, that all inspiration comes from the 'higher self' and therefore there are no guides, discarnate beings, intelligences from other spheres, other than little old us! Logically one might ask, if this is so, is there no point in cosmic consciousness where all those 'higher selves' communicate with each other, or are we supposed to be islands unto ourselves? The answer is, of course, that inspiration does not come entirely from ourselves, either higher or lower, for there is a pool of universal mind which accommodates all intelligences from every evolutionary sphere throughout the cosmos and it is possible to tune in to this and thus experience communication with, and inspiration from, minds outside our own.

Agreed there are many meditators who don't get much further than their own subconscious mind, but really the 'it's all me' syndrome is a bit of an ego trip if you care to think about it and, in essence, it denies the continuity of the soul or spirit into eternity. But then that is only my view for what it is worth (and I should say, in all honesty, the teaching of those who keep me on the straight and narrow!).

Occultists over many centuries have been advised to 'know, dare, be silent'; therefore to those anxious souls who seem to spend so much time searching for the secrets of the universe and getting nowhere very fast I say, 'Always remember the old eastern axiom: "when the chela/pupil is ready the guru appears"'.

First Psychic Steps

Let us now take those first psychic steps with the beginner and see what he or she is likely to encounter, how to recognize it, and how to effect a protection or some form of control over the process. A popular method today is to explore the subconscious mind, using a meditational technique that involves creative imagination. For example, one is asked to visualize, say, a green field, then extend the picture by looking to see what lies around or ahead. It may be the ocean, a cave in the mountain, a small dwelling or even a hole in the ground. When activated, the imagery processes in the brain will produce results varying with each individual and, if there is some deeper imbalance that is not outwardly obvious, this inward searching will soon bring it to the surface.

An old soul (whom I was once privileged to study under), likened those early steps along the occult path to looking for a gas leak with a lighted match. But this is the case with all consciousness-widening techniques, be they hypnotherapy, general psychic development, psychoanalysis, and so on, any of which can produce an abreaction if the wrong button (or the right one, perhaps) is touched off.

Most fairly well adjusted persons are able to use the codes of symbology to link them with their subconscious mind, whence they can proceed onwards and outwards into timelessness. Many terms are employed to describe that aspect of the self which takes over during these excursions into the field of universal thought: over-conscious, higher self, over soul, inner self; and so on. In fact, we are not a series of different people but one complete unit, although that unit is but a fragment of the group soul and the group soul, in turn, is but a fragment of the cosmos.

When we incarnate, only a very small portion or aspect of that unit is able to manifest. Let us liken it to a large tank of water, the spiritual whole, from which a few drops have been filtered into a tiny glass bottle — our body with its brain — and yet the water in the tank is in turn only a drop in the ocean of cosmic consciousness. The human brain is designed with the potential for contacting 'outer time' (some say 'inner space' which I find something of a contradiction of terms when one is dealing with a timeless and infinite universe), but there is a right time in the evolutionary cycle of every individual for doing this. If we try before that time is at hand, we will either get nowhere and end up saying there is no such thing and that it is all fakery, or we will find ourselves unable to compute what we encounter on our voyages into 'outer time' and end up with a mental breakdown.

But let us return to our student who is on the right lines, has progressed through his creative imagery across the green field into a cave (the subconscious) and entered a room where he comes face to face with a person, animal, flower, or symbol. In the language of symbology, this will furnish the trained observer with a great deal of knowledge about the student. To encounter the image of a person, for example, can indicate meeting with another aspect of one's self, i.e. the *anima/animus*, or it can symbolize a connecting with the group soul, twin soul or archetypal god-form which balances the spiritual personality; flowers and animals also have their language.

The skilled occultist or therapist can soon ascertain what they are dealing with and how best to help the developer or meditator to help themselves; but of course all persons taking groups for meditation are not so highly skilled or trained. Many people wish to pursue this type of study in the solitude of their own room and for these people there are also sets of rules, a highway code for safety-first if you like, which we shall examine.

CHAPTER TWO

OCCULT LAWS

Travelling the dimensions of outer time can be likened to travelling the network of thoroughfares stretching across our country. There are narrow lanes, busy city streets, cycle paths, woodland tracks, fast motorways; or one can always take a flight. On each of these avenues the dangers to be encountered are different and therefore the type of accident likely to happen will vary. Colliding with another cyclist might well cause a fracture, but the probability of breaking more than a bone upon collision with another vehicle travelling at 30 mph is much higher. The pedestrian taking a stroll through the woods might not encounter a double-decker bus but the local mugger could be on the loose. Travelling full speed in a fast sports car along an open motorway renders one extremely vulnerable to serious hurt or even death in the event of an accident, while few are lucky enough to survive an air crash! In other words, the dangers are relative to the conditions and activities, which is why 'L' drivers are not allowed on fast motorways and cyclists and pedestrians are required to avoid certain thoroughfares.

In psychic and occult work one usually only encounters the dangers associated with each stage of development as taken in the logical sequence of initiation. So, as long as one does not make the mistake of trying to run before one can crawl, the natural mechanisms of the brain can usually cope with any new impressions fed to it by the psyche expanding into altered states of consciousness. The student occultist encounters his or her initiations in a natural way, and it is a mistake to look for the way-out and phenomenal in psychic, occult or mystical development.

At one particularly difficult stage in my life, when everything seemed to be in a state of turmoil, the master with whom I was studying informed me that I was due for a major initiation. I recall thinking to myself, 'Oh no, not on top of everything else. . . .' But I ploughed on in desperation and was soon at the end of my tether, so I approached my master with all the humility I could muster and told him I had reached my limitation and could go no further, in which case I could never cope with the impending initiation. I recall his words: 'But, my dear, you have just passed it!' In fact, those very stressful conditions through which I had dragged myself in the preceding weeks were the initiation, whereas I was anxiously anticipating bumps in the night, occult enemies attacking me, black mental states and so forth. So, lesson number one, initiations crop up in ANY AREA OF LIFE that can teach us something, and not necessarily in psychic or occult form.

Occult Laws
There are a series of laws which are broadly termed 'occult', or relating to matters psychic or metaphysical. Two of these are applicable to psychic self-defence: THE LAW OF CHALLENGE and THE LAW OF EQUALITIES.

The law of challenge is used, or should be used, in all psychic or occult work and consists in placing a protection around oneself, or one's psychic charges, before commencing a working and CHALLENGING whatever puts in an appearance or makes itself or its presence felt. This challenge will vary with the school, tradition or system of occultism or religious belief adhered to by those participating.

In the early days of development, most of us are usually hung up on one particular belief or system, depending on our ethnic background and environmental programming. The most popular 'leaning post' in the west is the Christian tradition. It is amazing how many students rush back to what they feel to be the secure arms of the cross when they sense any form of psychic danger. I know one person who claims high estate in Wicca but who hastens back to Jesus when the wind whistles a little too freely through the trees! Well, this is all very well if you truly believe in Jesus, which is what I am trying to say. Protection is ultimately in the mind of the individual and if YOU believe a certain prayer or symbol will protect you then it will, UNLESS the next occult law, THE LAW OF EQUALITIES, comes into play.

The law of equalities decrees that if two minds cross in battle, or throw up opposing forces at each other (same thing, different way of putting it), one will gain ascendancy and thus pass a further initiation, while the other must stay down for a while longer and consolidate. Depending upon the intentions of the victor, there could also be wider considerations, but this is not an occult textbook so I'll simply clarify a little further by saying that if you are a student aspiring to the path and you cross swords with someone further up the ladder than yourself, you cannot hope to knock them out by simply waving a cross in front of them and ordering them off (with due apologies to a well known film company)!

I recall, some years ago when I was running a series of popular meetings in London, a young boy of about seventeen put in an appearance and after the talk approached me with the request, 'Could you please put me in touch with a really bad black magic group?'

'Whatever for?' I enquired, somewhat taken aback. 'Well,' he continued, 'I've read in this book that, if one takes along a crucifix and holds it up, the power of the Church will knock them all out and good will triumph over evil.' Oh, the optimism of youth. . . . If only it were that simple the world would be a kinder, gentler and more peaceful place in which to live! But sadly it does not work that way.

Just as my own initiation took place in the course of everyday existence so it is with the battle for light on this planet. Of course there are groups of mentally sick people (I refuse to hear them termed 'occultists') who indulge in cruel and foul rites, but the evils of mankind are far more generally perpetrated through the avenues of normal existence and in the day-to-day sufferings, privations, cruelties, sickness and fears of our age. There is an old Chinese saying, 'destined enemies always meet in narrow passages', and this is very true of the law of equalities.

So my advice to the student is to keep within his bounds and not go out looking for trouble. Take one step at a time and consolidate as you go, pausing at frequent intervals to 'earth' yourself. One of the greatest dispellers of fear is laughter and, as long as it is not at the expense of someone else or likely to cause embarrassment or suffering, do laugh off any fears. A wise old psychic once said to me many years ago, 'You know, old Nick hates to hear laughter,' and experience has certainly confirmed this.

Initiation

At this juncture it is as well to establish exactly what we mean by the term 'initiation'. Of course it is not a set of exams one passes, there are no psychic or occult 'A' levels. How I see initiation is like this: one embarks upon a course of study, not necessarily involving books and rites (although these may help), but being more concerned with producing an expansion of consciousness. As one progresses one slowly ascends to the next level. Perhaps it is erroneous to use the term 'ascends' as this implies a move upwards and one ultimately needs to expand in all directions through time and space. So shall we say 'arrives at a new level of awareness'? This has the effect of presenting the mind with a whole new series of experiences to compute, rationalize and place in perspective. It is when the mind, or psyche, cannot come to terms with what it has experienced that the initiation is failed, and the person is obliged to retreat to a former level where he feels safe and secure.

Which brings us right back to the question of what constitutes a safe haven, according to one's belief. Ultimately, the initiated soul will stand away from all systems and develop a reliance upon its own inner resources and unique personal understanding of the Great Universal Architect, Ultimate, Centre Point in Time, God, or whatever name you choose to call that state of all light. But if students attempt to assume the attributes of such a stage of spiritual awareness without first having ascended the ladder of initiation they will find themselves in trouble, and only a practitioner more advanced than themselves (the law of equalities) will be able to help them back on to their feet again.

CHAPTER THREE

HOW TO STRENGTHEN THE AURA

Every living thing has an aura, which is an energy or force field surrounding its physical shell. This aura acts as a protective guard against many things, including disease, the impingement of other minds or intelligences, it ensures the retaining of natural physical and mental energies, and so on. If our auras are damaged in some way, impurities can enter with dire results. I worked for many years in the field of healing and saw ample evidence of this. People who had sustained severe falls (which displaced the aura), often showed signs of other diseases in the ensuing months, always in places where the aura had been broken or put out of gear. Equally the aura will show the experienced occultist, or the psychic or mediumistic person, what is wrong with somebody who is sick and cannot be diagnosed by normal clinical methods. The aura shows discolorations, breaks, dents, and so on, when there is mental or physical sickness, and the colour (or lack of it) will help the healer to sum up the condition.

With psychic development the head aura tends to expand and is greatly in evidence with very advanced or 'old' souls. This is why saints or holy persons are often depicted with a halo around their head and even a shaft of light descending into that halo from above. Those of us who have worked with genuine trance mediums will have experienced seeing exactly the same phenomenon when an entity or intelligence of light sends its impulses into the mind of the medium through his or her head aura.

The aspiring psychic or occultist must therefore first of all learn to control his aura, so that he does not allow other minds to impinge upon it. There is an old saying, 'if you pull the devil's tail he will squeak', which really means, as I have already said, that if you do good in this world or bring light you will disturb the dark corners and send the 'nasties' scurrying in all directions. So anyone entering the mind-opening field is likely to come up against some opposition at some time. Learning to strengthen the aura will help to dispel unwanted influences and here are a few tips for the beginner on how to achieve this.

Auric Control
The aura, being of a finer substance or frequency than matter, functions at the same level or speed as thought. It is therefore controllable by thought processes; in other words, you can 'think' your aura open or closed at will. Not all that easy at first, though, rather like riding a bicycle, which looks so simple when the six-year-old next

door does it. But for the adult mounting the saddle for the first time, the question of balance can be difficult and the falls painful.

Here is a simple technique using colour. The safest and purest colours for auric use are blue and white. Now we all know what a large plastic bag looks like, the sort we use for our laundry or dry cleaning to keep out dust or dirt. Simply imagine you are stepping into a clear blue or clear white one, pulling it over your whole body and fastening it securely over the top of your head. But your mental plastic bag will be waterproof, germproof and astral-bullet-proof, if you see what I mean; and you will be able to see through it out into the world without being aware of it being there once it is in position. With regard to fastening it on the top, here you can use a safety-first symbol according to your personal persuasion. If you are a Christian you may like to think of a gold or silver cross. A Taoist may prefer the yin-yang symbolism; a Qabalist one of the sephira, the Hermeticist a caduceus; and so on.

If the idea of modern plastic displeases you, a cloak of a pure colour or clear light will work just as well. I recall as a child seeing a statue of the Virgin Mary robed in a heavenly blue garment covering her from her feet upwards and slowly merging into a silver diadem of stars around her head. A lovely auric coverage, this, but if you are one of those macho gentlemen who fight shy of the feminine principle (shame, as you'll have to come to terms with it sooner or later), what about a suit of shining armour complete with Athenian helmet? After all, this Greek goddess was the strongest of all warriors, triumphing even over Ares, god of war, himself. But unlike Ares, who fought for pleasure, Athene only fought to defend, and therein lies an occult truth. . . .

So, you see, learning to control the aura and keeping it closed at all times is not very difficult, simply a question of controlling your mind. After a while the action becomes automatic and you will find that you can expand and contract your aura at will. An experienced occultist or psychic, not wishing to advertise his presence when entering a room, can draw his aura in, or 'mask' as we call it, as it is not always advisable to play one's aces. The colour of the aura may change during different stages of development, but it is advisable to avoid any agitatory colours in the head region during psychic workings or occult rites. And if you notice that someone you are working with is producing bright reds or dirty brown colours around the head region, close yourself down immediately and if possible break the circle.

Whites, blues, certain shades of green or pale lilac are acceptable in the head aura during periods of psychic activity and, if you notice gold or silver, then all the better. Do remember, it is YOUR MIND that controls your aura. Healers may cleanse it for you and help you to rebuild it after periods of sickness or initiation, but as with your body, it is YOUR personal vehicle and how you treat it once you have that knowledge is between you and Maat (the Egyptian goddess of truth who weighs the hearts of men against the feather of truth in the halls of Osiris after the death of the body, according to the Egyptian tradition).

CHAPTER FOUR

SYMBOLS FOR COSMIC PROTECTION

Just as there are safety first codes on our highways and byways, so there are certain symbols that help us to take safe passage through the realms of extended consciousness. In Egyptian magic Anubis, son of Nephthys (psychism) and Osiris (light and truth), was assured of complete safety in negotiating that underworld equated with what many psychics and occultists call the lower astral. One must remember that what we are dealing with in occultism is principles and not personalities, and Anubis represents just such a principle.

It is often easier for many of us to visualize a principle in form than in the abstract; hence the jackal-like Anubis, or Cerberus guarding the gates of the Greek Hades.

The Egyptian magi were telling us that truth and light are necessary torches to bear if we are aiming to negotiate the realms of psychism with safety, and we must therefore cultivate the Anubis within us in order to emerge from the twilight zones in one piece. Interesting to note that Anubis was also lord of anaesthetics (the spirit out of the body) and patron of psychiatrists and psycho-analysts! The same principles apply in all these practices and, in astrology, Anubis equates with the planet Pluto.

The symbols used for protection will, as I have emphasized, depend very much upon the persuasion of the user UNLESS YOU ARE ABLE TO DISCOVER YOUR PERSONAL AND GOD SYMBOLS, which are just as safe, if not safer, than most others. But for those who feel happier sheltering beneath the umbrella of orthodoxy I will enumerate a few 'safe' symbols from different systems and beliefs; any of these can be used prior to meditation, psychic development or occult rites as a form of invocatory protection, the idea being that they automatically tune the user into the originator of that particular belief, or draw from the stock-pile of thought and prayer built up by that religion over the ages.

SYMBOLOGY

CHRISTIAN	Christ cross, rose, chalice or graal, dove.
EGYPTIAN	Ankh, *djed* or column of Osiris, eye of Horus, throne of Isis.
NORSE	The runes $\langle$ Υ $\sqrt{}$
QABALISTIC	Sephira 1 (Kether) or 6 (Tiphereth). Pentacle with point upwards.
TAROT	Nos. 1 & 2 together (the Magician & High Priestess) or Nos. 9 & 11 together (the Hermit & Strength).
PANTHEISTIC	Elemental symbols (fire, air, water and earth), equal armed cross, oak tree.

EASTERN   There are many different schools of mysticism within the eastern tradition, each with its own deities and associated symbologies. For beginners not aiming to master the occult path I would recommend that they stay with the yin-yang symbol or the simple white four- or six-petalled lotus. The multi-petalled lotus is associated with the sahasrara chakra, so it is best to leave this one until the passage of the kundalini through the lower chakras has been mastered. Certain popular mantras may be suitable for the ethnic groups or cultures in which they flowered, but are not necessarily right for the westerner.

There are many other occult schools or traditions, each with its own protective symbol, and numerous variations of the ones I have already given, but to cover them all would take a book in itself. Ultimately the student should seek his own personal and God symbols, as these will not tie him to any existing system but allow him free rein to establish direct contact with his true cosmic links or archetypal roots.

Personal and God Symbols

Each and every individual has a symbol which is personal to him or her. It may be some simple object such as a white flower, a yellow ribbon, a star form, an animal, a blade of grass, ANYTHING AT ALL. Never dismiss an impression because it may seem too mundane, as all is permitted. It is quite possible that someone else may have a similar symbol to yourself; this does not matter and simply indicates a group soul connection.

The Method: Your last real contact with outer time, and therefore with your subconscious mind in its purest form free from environmental programming, was just prior to your conception, so this is what you do:

SEAT YOURSELF COMFORTABLY, OR YOU CAN LIE DOWN IF YOU WISH. Close your eyes and imagine yourself taking a journey backward through time to the moment of your birth. Re-enter the womb and emerge at the other end at the point of your actual conception just prior to entering the embryo that is to become you. Pause for one moment and then start to move forward again in time, passing through the drama of your birth and, as you so do, imagine you are taking hold of a silver cord from your baby form and pulling it along with you as you proceed forward towards the present.

Pass through the experiences of childhood, pausing here and there to register some particularly traumatic or meaningful event, great happiness, pain or new awareness and each time you pause, MAKE A KNOT IN YOUR SILVER CORD. Continue travelling mentally through your teenage years forward to whichever part of your life you have now reached, BUT ALWAYS PAUSING TO IMBIBE THE SENSATIONS OF AN IMPORTANT EVENT AND KNOTTING YOUR CORD ACCORDINGLY.

And so you will arrive in present time, trailing your cord full of knots. Pull in the beginning of the cord towards you and join it to the end which represents the present, rather like the serpent eating its own tail (*ouroboros*). Thus a circle is created. Continuing to use your creative imagination, lay the circle flat and step into it. You will immediately find yourself sinking down as though through darkness, though not of a frightening nature. This circle represents the sum total of your experience as a spirit or psyche, as brought forward from your subconscious mind in outer time and added to in the present or inner time life.

Having allowed yourself to descend through the circle you will eventually find that you come to what feels like the bottom. The experience will vary with each individual, but it is often a muddy or watery base representing the primordial womb. Keep relaxed and breathe slowly and deeply and you will automatically start to rise again, BUT THE WAY IN WHICH YOU RISE WILL BE UNIQUE TO YOU. You may find yourself ascending a flight of stairs, or flying with wings, or climbing the side of a mountain, but whatever the method involved, you WILL ascend.

The first thing you 'see' when you reach the top of your 'well' or dark passage will be YOUR OWN PERSONAL SYMBOL. For example, you may find yourself plodding up a flight of seemingly never ending stairs and suddenly you come to the top and there is light from a window. Looking out of that window you see a tree in full blossom. That tree will be your PERSONAL SYMBOL. Or you may open a door that reveals a simple hat hanging on a peg. That hat will be your symbol.

Until you try you won't know, BUT IT MUST BE THE FIRST IMPRESSION THAT COMES TO YOU. No use trying several times because you see a woolly lamb the first time and feel you're not particularly keen on sheep, so you'll have another go and see if you can get a silver cross, which you'd much prefer. Perhaps the shepherd is your archetype and the sooner you come to terms with yourself and stop chasing the hierophantic archetype the better.

HAVING LEARNED YOUR TRUE SOUL OR PERSONAL SYMBOL, KEEP THIS IN MIND ALWAYS FOR SAFETY AS IT WILL LINK YOU WITH YOUR GROUP SOUL. VISUALIZE IT WHEN GOING TO SLEEP, WHEN FRIGHTENED OR TIRED, AND SO ON. THE NEXT SYMBOL YOU NEED TO KNOW IS YOUR GOD SYMBOL, WHICH IS YOUR ADDITIONAL PROTECTION BECAUSE IT REPRESENTS YOUR OWN PERSONAL LINK WITH THE CENTRAL FORCE OF THE UNIVERSE, WHETHER YOU CALL IT GOD, THE ULTIMATE, THE CENTRE POINT IN TIME, OR ANYTHING ELSE. YOUR PERSONAL SYMBOL IS THE DIVINE SPARK UNIQUE TO YOU, YOUR GOD SYMBOL IS THE CONNECTING LINK BETWEEN THAT SPARK AND THE WHOLE FIRE THAT IS THE INFINITE CREATOR.

Your God Symbol: Everyone has a God symbol or sacred archetype. This you may well share with others of your group soul, depending on the evolutionary stream or impulse from which you have originated.

The Method: Having fully familiarized yourself with your own personal symbol, relax in a meditative posture and visualize your personal symbol as strongly as you can. Enlarge it in your mind's eye until it becomes something in which you can sit: if it is a tree you may recline in its branches; if a swan, you may be seated on its back; a star, you may sit astride its points; a small child you may hold close to you; and so on. Feel absolutely secure in your hold, then proceed as follows: START TO ROTATE YOUR SYMBOL CLOCKWISE, SLOWLY AT FIRST BUT INCREASING IN MOTION AS YOU START TO SPIN.

Close your psychic eye so that you don't feel dizzy or giddy. You'll find you need to give the whole process a little push to start with, although some people who have tried this have set off in a swirling motion straight away with a minimum of mental effort. It does not matter how long it takes as this will vary with the individual. For a second or two you will spin, then you will slow down and come to a halt. You will, in fact, land somewhere in 'outer time'. You can then mentally look around you and the first thing you see will be your archetype, who will greet you or give you some point of reference.

For example, upon opening your psychic eye you may find yourself in a lush meadow where a lady wearing a blue gown and crowned with flowers comes forth to greet you. She may take the wreath of flowers from her head and present it to you. That will be your God symbol. NOTE, ALSO, THE NATURE OF THE BEING WHO GREETS YOU: IN YOUR TERMS OF REFERENCE IT COULD BE A GOD OR GODDESS OR EVEN A MOTHER, FATHER OR AVUNCULAR PERSON, but it will represent THE OTHER HALF OF YOUR NATURAL, SPIRITUAL POLARITY, the *anima/animus*, or active/passive as the case may be. Your spiritual polarity has no bearing on which sex you incarnate into in any life, as both principles can be expressed in male and female bodies.

Having now established your PERSONAL SYMBOL and your GOD SYMBOL, always use both when undertaking any psychic or occult work, especially in other time zones (past, future, and so on), AS THESE ARE YOUR SECURITY CODES AND WILL ENSURE YOU SAFE PASSAGE THROUGH THE UNFAMILIAR TERRITORIES OF ALTERED STATES OF CONSCIOUSNESS. One connects you with your group soul, the other with your source. These two disciplines are specially designed for those who have no particular belief or religious adherence and are every bit as efficacious, if not more so in many cases, as some of the so-termed 'safe passes' handed out by more conventional religious and psychic organizations and gurus.

Individual Protection

Many people do not care to work in a group or with others, but prefer to study, meditate and develop on their own. There are pros and cons to everything, of course, and psychic development is no exception. The lone developer may find himself in difficulties if a working, meditation or psychic probe misfires, and there's nothing so comforting as having somebody around who knows the ropes and can deal with unwanted influences and re-adjust one's aura after a psychic topple. But, on the other hand, when working alone one is less likely to encounter the sort of cross vibes from others which can be caused by moods, wrong thinking or negative emotions. The individual can develop alone but must be prepared to face up to his own decisions and sort out his own problems, as the path of inner development is NEVER entirely free of difficulties and it is through coping with these difficulties that the student learns and advances.

Having decided to work alone, the precautions to be taken are much the same as those you would need to observe if you were in a group although, having elected to accept responsibility for yourself, you would need to be absolutely sure of your procedures. Protection may be effected in one of two ways: (a) by disciplined thought processes; and (b) by employing protective ritual. Let us first of all examine (a).

It is a well-known fact that we only use a small part of our brain, but then our brain is little more than a computer, which sifts and decodes information passed to it by our mind. Confusion of terms often results from referring to brain, mind, spirit, subconscious, so a little qualifying is necessary at this stage.

Recent research on the human brain confirms its computer-like nature, with the left hemisphere dealing with inner time and the practical and mundane aspects of our life and the right hemisphere with imagery, creativity and outer time, as we have already discussed. Some scientists are of the opinion that we have no additional 'mind' or spirit but are simply motivated by our physical brain. This school of thought is known as 'monoism', while those researchers who subscribe to the theory that the brain is simply the tool of an abstract, non-physical intelligence (mind) are called dualists.

Experiments have shown how the two hemispheres of the brain can function independently of each other, but tests have also indicated that man can 'think' without the nuts and bolts of his brain being fully functional or even all present. The occultist naturally supports the theory of dualism, believing that the mind is the conscious expression of the psyche or spirit, that intelligence which imbibes information, observes, learns from experience and adds to the spiritual whole; the spirit is the real YOU, that fragment of your group soul which is exclusively unique but which is a complementary part or spark of the infinite fire or force of creation.

The term 'subconscious mind' is one of many that have surfaced via modern psychiatry and which probably relates to instinctive imagery as decoded by the brain's right hemisphere. It is usually associated with outer time; hence those hypnotherapy romps back to childhood on which analysts love to take their patients in the hope of triggering off the right set of co-ordinates for a successful abreaction. But, as psychiatry and medicine evolve, doubtless this term will end up in the Freudian or Jungian archives along with 'superconscious', 'libido' and a dictionary or more of similar words that have become commonplace in psychiatry over the past few decades.

CHAPTER FIVE

MIND OVER MATTER

Techniques known to the older civilizations for centuries have been used to effect the control of mind over matter. These may be evidenced among the mystical practices of India, Tibet and other Far Eastern countries as well as in the religions of the Middle East and Christian mysticism. They are matched in modern times by bio-feedback, the ability possessed by some people to change the atomic structure of metals and move objects by mental concentration. These techniques have been researched both in the Soviet Union and the West with astounding results. We do not have the space here to examine the evidence available, as our prime concern is mind power as a protective shield.

Thought precedes all action and the old axiom 'as above, so below' is never more true than in matters metaphysical. Therefore, if one is functioning at a level at which thought is the *primum mobile*, one must surely use that same force to negotiate its field? That is why the aura can be controlled by mind power; in other words, you can 'think' your aura closed, open, coloured this or that way, and so on, a line of logic that is of course allied to the subject of self-healing.

But few of us have minds disciplined enough to cope with anything too advanced, so simple procedures are best to start with. The individual embarking upon a lone psychic study or experiment is therefore advised to employ techniques of visualization for protection. This can commence with an auric build-up, followed by a thought protection which should extend well beyond the immediate body vicinity. Just as I explained how to effect a closed and protected aura, so that technique can be used to cover or protect a room. Some practitioners like to have a special room for meditation or development, which is fair enough if you can manage it, but — with accommodation at a premium these days — there are many who are forced to eat, live, sleep and carry out their mystical workings in the same room. So number one on the list is to clear the room of all unwanted vibrations.

Seat yourself cómfortably, build your aura mentally, make your imagery according to your belief, i.e. religious, occult or cosmic. Then imagine a shaft of pure light issuing from your protective symbol and slowly sweeping round the room. Always work clockwise (*deoshins*), sending your beam of light right round until every corner has been filled, and don't forget those areas directly above and below your room. Some people prefer to think of their room as becoming encased in a kind of protective bowl through which they can peer psychically at the universe beyond and, at the same time, be shielded from its less desirable influences.

Right. So we have relaxed, invoked our protective symbols, dealt with our own auras and cleansed our operating theatre. Then we can proceed to carry out whatever practice we have in mind. But what if things go wrong? Nasty influences have been known to penetrate even the most careful of defences, so how does one deal with the sudden intrusion of a very uncomfortable vibe? The first thing is to return immediately to a normal state of consciousness or, as my master used to say to me in the days before it was the done thing to employ the language of parapsychology, 'Get back into your body.'

Earth thoroughly, clear the atmosphere, once again using the beam of light technique, and CLOSE YOUR AURA. In fact, the aura should be checked and closed after a working of *any* kind, and that includes ALL trips into altered states of consciousness in any therapy. Returning to the conscious state too quickly can leave the patient or developing psychic with a fuzzy head, inability to concentrate, and a host of what are loosely described as 'withdrawal symptoms'. The same applies in the sleep state, when one is suddenly awakened from theta state by some extraneous noise. Most of my readers will have experienced a myoclonic jerk, the medical name given to that sudden jump the body can give if disturbed, an experience often accompanied by a dream of falling or walking down stairs and missing one!

If, after having closed your aura, cleared the room and done what you can, you still feel uncomfortable, you can call upon a higher force (again varying with your individual belief), or seek the aid of someone more experienced in the occult field, should the phenomenon continue. As I explained earlier, it all depends at what level you choose to operate as to which alien forces you are likely to encounter. Keep within your limits at any given stage and you will find it easy to cope on your own.

It is possible to create and dissolve thought-forms by using mind power, but such practices are applicable only to those who are making a serious study of the occult or magical path and should not be dabbled with by the beginner or early-stage loner.

On the subject of dabbling, what about those favourite experiments with ouija boards, planchettes and glasses on tables, which beginners seem drawn to? I am frequently asked what kind of force operates during such sessions. This will depend very much upon the sitters. If one of those participating is a natural medium, the instrument can be effectively moved by energies transmitted through them from a guide or interested discarnate entity. Equally, a psycho-kinetic energy can be generated which can be manipulated unconsciously by the mind of someone present, or a mischievous elementary spirit, or even an elemental, can take part in the game and direct the power so as to cause a nuisance or give a fright. Experiments of this kind undertaken by those who are not familiar with the cosmos, or outer time, frequently produce after-effects in the location where they have taken place. A close friend of mine noticed all sorts of strange phenomena in her home for some weeks after trying the tumbler technique. Safety measures or adequate precautions should always be applied when tuning into or trying to attract intelligences or energies from unseen dimensions, and no instance is too insignificant for this rule to apply. In ninety-nine per cent of cases there may be no ill effects, but there are the odd instances where the nuisance factor can become out of hand.

Protection Through Ritual
There are many people who feel much safer if they employ some form of ritual. Indeed the psychological need for a devotional outlet has been noted by psychiatrists and students of metaphysics alike. It appears that we each have a degree of religious potential within our make-up and how we choose to express this will vary according to our personal evolution and group soul experience. Rituals can evoke an emotional atmosphere engendering feelings of devotion.

The efficacy of all this will depend very much upon the faith and sincerity of those employing the system. The sincere believer will automatically tune himself into the collective thought force of the faith he follows, which will open up for him a storehouse of power. But although this may sound all very nice and safe, and as often as not give a feeling of elation and mystical fulfilment, it is as well to bear in mind that the power is LIMITED TO THAT PARTICULAR MANIFESTATION OF FAITH and does not ultimately offer anything like the potential available to those who are prepared to stop strap-hanging and step directly into the timeless zones of the cosmos.

Religious and occult systems of the past have usually made their appearance at a time in our planet's evolution when it was necessary for man's mind to be drawn into this or that form of spiritual discipline. They therefore carry the stamp or hallmark of the age in which they were first manifest. But we have now entered the Aquarian Age, the age of individual responsibility. So while it may well be a good thing to use the classroom textbooks as a basis, if only because their terms of reference suffice for communication purposes, ultimately we must leave school and realize our position as cosmic citizens, not simply denizens of tribal earth.

Those wishing to employ ritualistic methods for protection should seek out a good textbook dealing with the particular system of their choice. One piece of advice at this juncture: DO NOT MIX SYSTEMS. There are such things as rays and anti-rays (which I shall deal with shortly) and if you invoke energies that are not compatible, you may soon end up with psychological problems, if not material ones to boot!

For the average westerner the Qabalah is a tried and tested traditional system, and I have always found the Greek tradition safe and easy to handle. Not always the Egyptian system, however, which can disagree violently with some people, although for those who can master it there is a wealth of knowledge and wisdom to be gained from it. Norse magic is excellent for the more earthy among us, and the Hermetic path will suit the intellectual. Pantheism can be homely and comforting as long as its adherents are fully familiar with the functions of the muladhara chakra and know how to cope if the kundalini gets hooked up at that junction.

But when it comes to the eastern systems which have become so popular of late, there are dangers. The westerner has been schooled to a more active and practical approach to life, and the passivity of some eastern mystical approaches can tend to unbalance him and put him out of gear with the world around him if he is not careful. Some of you may well argue that this might not be such a bad thing, but if you have worked for many years with mental illness, as I did, you will realize that becoming out of harmony with the other fragments of your group soul and with your cosmic origins creates psychic tensions and does not make for happiness or balance, either in spiritual seeking or everyday life.

Psychic and occult experimenters often think it is clever to 'have a go' at one system one evening and another the next. One ray can cancel out another, while energies can be generated which could prove unmanageable. So, if you want a change, make a complete break. Erect your pentacle with appropriate Qabalistic protective symbols if you honestly believe that this will do the trick but, should you become bored with it and fancy something different, don't leap straight into the Egyptian system as the two are *not* compatible. Move over to Pantheism, Celtic magic or even Christian mysticism. Don't embark upon a course of Tibetan *bon* and mix it with crucifixes and the trappings of western Christianity; like oil and water, they do not mix. Proceed slowly through each method if you must switch over, and use a good bridging system such as Atlantean occultism, which provides a meeting point between eastern and western traditions.

Protection for the Group
Group leaders who accept responsibility for the development and psychic safety of others should be especially careful as they are involving themselves in the karmic pattern of the lives of their charges. An inexperienced group leader can do untold harm to those in his care by directing them into unfamiliar psychic territories, wherein they are unable to cope. Furthermore, such leaders lack the experience or know-how to set their pupils back again into their right cosmic orbits. Physical and mental illness can result from dabbling in altered states of consciousness without knowing how to re-earth so, those of you who fancy yourselves as budding gurus, beware the wheel of karma.

The procedures for dealing with group protection are much the same as for the individual, except that the leader must effect the cover in the meeting place and also check out his or her charges. At the end of a session he

should ensure that everyone he is responsible for is
properly earthed, has a closed aura and has not collected
any undesirable 'auric-limpets', thought-forms or
unwelcome entities during the process. Obviously the best
way is to instruct those participating to effect the
disciplines for themselves.

Some group leaders like to work through prayers or
mantras, and in meditation circles in particular these can
be most effective and induce a harmonious atmosphere.
But, remember, subtle energies should never be invoked
unless utilized in some way, or some member of the outfit
gifted with ESP will probably find himself enveloped in a
vortex of power that could result in more than the
discomfort of a sleepless night! All energies generated
MUST be placed. If your group is unsure as to what to do
with a build-up of power, healing is always a good and
ethical outlet, and peace and harmony for the planet as a
whole are top spiritual priorities. Of course it all depends
on what your group is 'into'. Some may like to send out
their accumulated thought power to help animals,
ecology, the elemental kingdoms, sick or ignorant people
or a variety of sociological causes. That, group leader, is
your concern, just as it is up to the individual working
alone to select his target. I cannot pontificate on the
ethics of any cause. I can only advise that it be selfless and
constructive, in keeping with the forward directional
impulses of cosmic law.

The normal meditational exercises in body
consciousness are excellent, both for relaxation prior to a
working, and earthing after you have finished. For those
unfamiliar with the technique, it consists of sitting in a
relaxed position and, commencing with the toes, tensing
them and then relaxing them, then the ankles, calves,
knees, thighs, tummy, and so on, right up to the head. At
the finish it helps the 'earthing' if a person can again
become aware of all parts of his body and the full
functioning processes of the motor-nervous system.

Many people suffer feelings of disassociation after
meditation or psychic work. Group leaders should never

allow a person to wander off in this state. A warm drink, conversation, and a good straightening up of the aura all help to put things right. It will be the more sensitive among the group who will be subject to this sort of condition, but there is a fine line between mental instability and psychic perception, which I shall deal with in detail shortly.

CHAPTER SIX

PSYCHIC ATTACKS

Meditation is very much the 'in' thing today. People are told that the alpha brain pattern induced by meditative practices is greatly beneficial, both mentally and physically, and therefore they should spend a certain period each day in meditation. There are many forms of meditation, not all of which are, in my opinion, suited to people from western cultures.

Meditation undertaken alone can be perfectly safe as long as the individual concerned knows his or her basic highway code of protection. In other words, the same rules apply as with those wishing to probe psychically or occultly on their own. But there are many who feel more comfortable if they can meditate in a group.

Some months back I was asked to lead a group meditation of this kind at a major London festival. People paid a small sum to attend and the procedure was simply to fill the room each time and those who couldn't be fitted in waited for the next session. I therefore found myself faced with a cross-section of the public, some of whom were experienced meditators and students of matters occult, and others who had just dropped in to see what it was all about. Difficult, but not insurmountable.

It is possible to lead a meditation that is safe for a mixed group. This is simply achieved by the use of protective archetypal symbols which will slot each individual into his correct psychic groove. I used the 'creative imagination' technique, but kept a close watch on everyone, just to make sure that no one experienced any difficulties. Some entered quite deep states of trance, while others were more mentally alert and, when I wound the session up and brought everyone back to earth, there were one or two who needed to be helped to regain a full state of consciousness. I drew in their auras and sealed them off safely so that there were no side effects when they left the room. But I have heard of many instances where this has not been done, simply because the group leader did not possess the 'know how'. Consequently, one or two of the extra-sensitive people were left in a dazed state and with their auras wide open.

An open aura can attract all sorts of influences, just as a candle attracts moths and, if some mental imbalance does result, the medical practitioner or psychiatrist who ends up with the case might feel quite justified in saying that all mystic practices are conducive to mental stress or the deterioration of the psyche. So, those of you who undertake the responsibility of leading open meditations, DO ensure that the trusting folk who have placed themselves under your protection are not let down.

Drugs and Artificial Stimulants

Psychic, occult or meditative work should never be undertaken while under the influence of any form of artificial stimulus. During induced trips the consciousness is forced open sideways, as it were. The experimenter does not really take in anything that is not already within his or her existing terms of reference. Brilliant colours, lovely landscapes, visions of Buddha, Christ, angels, spacemen, all are familiar reference points in the history of human consciousness. If something is experienced which the subconscious mind lacks the terms of reference to express, some abstract symbol may surface, but what many trippers do not realize is, that with a little mental discipline and the correct training, they may sample — at no cost — any of the psychedelia of a good acid or pot trip, plus many more wonders of the universe, and effect a positive control over the bad journeys!

Certain drugs actually damage the brain cells and, as any occultist knows, it is difficult for the spirit or psyche to function accurately through faulty physical mechanisms. It can be rather like losing a finger or damaging a toe; the balance of the body is affected and a new set of muscles has to be brought into play so that normal functioning can be restored. A brain that is damaged or surgically altered can compensate to a certain degree, as recent experiments in brain surgery have shown, but there comes a point where co-ordination is impaired and the type of clear thinking necessary for metaphysical work is beyond the sufferer.

In addition to the possibility of causing bad trips, any artificial stimulant, from pep pills to alcohol, is not good for psychic, occult or mystical work, and studies undertaken under these conditions tend to give a slightly distorted view which will not provide a firm foundation for genuine and spiritually ethical cosmic development. I don't much care whose toes I tread on here for my conscience dictates that this has to be clearly and categorically stated.

While on the subject of psychic self-defence, where the dangers can come from sources other than obvious occult ones, what about subliminal projection? I am given to understand that some pop cults are using messages written backwards in songs to influence people's minds. They sound quite normal when heard consciously, but played backwards they have revealed sinister messages and instructions which the subconscious mind (or right hemisphere of the brain) can decode and possibly act upon without understanding why. This is much more 'black magic' in the true sense than a few sexually frustrated folk dancing round a cauldron on midsummer's eve. Readers should bear in mind that the powers of evil are not past using the aids of modern science to perpetrate their foul deeds; so it does nobody,

psychic or otherwise, any harm to observe a few
precautionary rules.

What Constitutes a Psychic Attack?

Where does imagination end and genuine psychic
experience begin? Some years ago, when I was working
with an occult healing group, I was called to investigate
the case of a lady who claimed to be possessed by an evil
entity. A lot of fuss was being made of her and she
welcomed me warmly with a request to 'take away the
nasty spirit which is causing me to be such a dreadful
person'. After I had quieted her down and talked to her I
discovered that when this 'other being' took over she
became abusive to those around, telling them in no
uncertain terms what she thought of them and
complaining in the ripest of language about anything
that displeased her.

I recall standing over her and scanning her aura.
There was nothing there! No offending spook lurked
nearby, no evil entity was attached, and all I could pick
up were signs of stress and some slight mental imbalance.
After further questions it didn't take me long to work out
that I was dealing with a lady who had read a few books
about possessions and saw the idea as a good excuse to say
what she really had on her mind without accepting
responsibility for her words or actions. When she wanted
to scold her aunt, but didn't dare, it was so easy to be
rude and place the blame on some fictitious spirit; and
she soon discovered that a few well aimed remarks, plus
offensive language, produced faster and more desirable
results when she wanted her own way than a quiet plea in
her normal manner. A suppressed aspect of her self was
surfacing and had become slightly out of control, nothing
more. I explained this to those who were caring for her
and diplomatically faced her with it. After breaking
down she admitted she had always felt put upon and
pushed around to a point where she could take no more.
It was then that the 'entity' had made its appearance.
Fortunately it disappeared from then on, never to return,

but she did learn to be more positive, and her loved ones also realized their mistake and paid more heed to her needs.

Unfortunately the balance between genuine psychic or mystical experience and mental illness is a delicate one. What makes matters worse is that the mentally sick are so often attracted to the psychic or occult field, usually because being with others who claim paranormal experiences gives them a sense of being less of an 'odd man out'.

When I first started taking an interest in these things, I was taken to a well-known London establishment and introduced around. I was in my early twenties at the time and found myself in the minority for my age group. On that first evening alone I was approached by four different people who all assured me, in the strictest confidence, that they were great masters travelling incognito through life. Less stouter hearts might have fled the spot, never to return, but I was undaunted. A very close associate of mine also visited the same organization and encountered four 'Jesus Christs' in one evening!

It is little wonder that the medical profession generally tends to frown on anything hinting at matters mystical or occult, although of late the climate of establishment opinion has mellowed considerably with the spread of interest in fringe medicine, or 'alternative therapies' as they are now referred to.

Of course it can be argued that the mentally unstable should never be let loose in a psychic atmosphere, but who is to prevent this? And how do we know who should or shouldn't have a go? A study of the birth chart will always give a good clue as to a person's suitability or otherwise. An easy chart does not make for a good occultist as it tends to produce a character that will have difficulty in coping with the inevitable stresses and oppositions to be encountered along the path of truth. A certain amount of tension in a chart is necessary as long as it is not of the sort that could cause a mental explosion (or implosion in some cases) or any form of withdrawal, and the ability to earth quickly and securely is a 'must'.

Good aspects to Mercury will ensure a clear thinking and balanced mind; Venus well placed gives the ability to harmonize with others; and afflictions between Uranus, Neptune and Moon should be watched for. An over-active imagination (Moon) can often be confused with the psychic gift, and the pity is that such individuals often set themselves up as clairvoyants or public helpers of some kind. Little wonder that many clients claim to have been told a lot of rubbish. Somewhere along the line the over-imaginative — but not truly psychic — person might accidentally hit upon a truth, which could sell them for quite a considerable run before things catch up with them.

So what IS a genuine psychic or occult attack, and is there really such a thing? What is referred to as a psychic attack is usually an instance where the mind of the student, be he pursuing the occult, psychic or mystical path, comes into opposition with a force, energy or intelligence either not on his particular wavelength or actually 'anti' the frequency of his group soul or evolving impulse and therefore 'anti' him. As the universe is composed of an infinite number of frequencies in all and every conceivable permutation, chances of this occurring at some time or other are quite high.

When coming into contact with an alien force, either accidentally unfriendly (simply a matter of vibes which do not gel and no implications of evil intent) or definably hostile, the law of equalities immediately comes into play. A battle of minds ensues and the victor emerges the wiser for the encounter, albeit with a few bruises or wounds to lick. The vanquished proceeds on its way and adjusts its sights in the light of *its* experience.

These encounters with incompatible forces or energies can crop up at any time, day or night, and in any circumstances. Nor are they limited to the world of phenomena, as they can just as easily rear their ugly heads in the form of a new boss at work, an evil-tongued scandalmonger or an unjust legal decision. Sometimes the effects can be purely mental but equally they can be physical, affecting health or even money flow, housing, job, emotional commitments, and so on. HOW one adjusts to them is the deciding factor in one's further metaphysical development, and it is as well to bear in mind that not all of us can go all the way, or even half the way, towards the goal to which we may have originally aspired. 'Know thyself' is very important; it means to know one's archetype and therefore one's *modus operandi* of psychic functioning.

One of the great mistakes so often made by beginners in this field is to pin normal day-to-day stresses on occult sources. The average person or man in the street — is there such an animal? Maybe not, but you know what I mean — has his ups and downs. He gets a toothache on Monday, makes a dental appointment for Tuesday, only to find to his annoyance that he has been double booked. On Wednesday he enjoys a comparatively trouble-free day but on Thursday, oh dear, the exhaust falls off his car and the sewer gets blocked. Friday sees him falling out with his girl friend, on Saturday he 'drinks it off' with the boys, while on Sunday his lady rings to say she's sorry. The following week he gets his car fixed, his tooth attended to, everything is put right and heigh ho we're off again on another path of trivia.

There is a fine dividing line between everyday pressures and occult interference, and students of the path should realize that they will not be exempted from the normal flow of things, simply because they are seeking beyond the banalities of everyday existence. But, on the other hand, the tests will come in the areas of highest vulnerability, and we all have our Achilles heel.

I am always highly suspicious of those occult students who claim to have been transfixed by the gaze of some black magician on the London Underground, with the result that they end up with a ghastly headache. By the law of averages, I suppose, one *could* bump into a 'nasty' on a public service vehicle, but in my own experience I haven't found it to be this way; and that goes for many people I have trained or who have passed through my hands over the years. But then, as the saying goes, a fear is an unrequited wish. . . .

People are going to form relationships, fall in and out of love, conceive children (or not, as the case may be), move house, obtain a good job or get the sack, regardless of occult goings on, all these things being part of the rich patterns of karma that are the signposts of our existence. Mental illness may not be obvious to the untrained, or even to the trained person initially, but close and careful observation will soon show up the cracks and, if the match of knowledge is not kept well away from any open gas leaks, as sure as eggs are eggs there will be a big bang! And who picks up the pieces? Usually the medical profession or those who practise alternative therapies.

So, dear student (and dear teacher), watch for those little tell-tale signs and, remember, the best psychic or occultist is not necessarily the most eccentric, neither does the truly advanced student carry a banner or advertise his presence; he simply does not need to.

Science and Psychism
The Aquarian Age is said to be the time when mystical knowledge, which was formerly the specific area of occultists and priests, comes out into the open and is rationalized by science. It has been described as the meeting place for physics and metaphysics, psychology and parapsychology, and so on. A whole dictionary of reference has been built up over the past few years incorporating such terms as ESP (extra sensory perception), ASC (altered states of consciousness), OOBE (out-of-the-body experiences), prescience and so forth, many of which are now in common use, even within the sheltered bastions of orthodoxy.

Old spooky terms, like ghosts, psychic gifts, visions, clairvoyance, are out; and yet it is still difficult to convey occult or psychic matters in scientific terms without sounding like a suitable case for treatment! No doubt as time progresses these problems will be overcome and scientists will reach some agreement regarding the terms of reference employed in metaphysics and the validity of supernormal claims, using their own methodology; and so a standard will be formed and accepted.

Most of us have heard about the four different types of brainwaves, BETA — our active, conscious, thinking, awake lives; ALPHA — a relaxed state as emphasized in meditation techniques; THETA — that state of drowsiness, near unconsciousness, dreamlike, when time is suspended and reality becomes blurred; and DELTA, which involves deep sleep. That these states can be artificially induced is also accepted by science and although alpha patterns may be all very nice when one is sitting cross-legged contemplating one's navel, they are hardly appropriate if one is driving a car and is drawn into them by traffic signals flashing at certain intervals as has been recently observed

In other words, there is a natural time and place for everything. For example, theta emissions are ideal for psychic development and astral projection, and alpha for meditation, relaxation and some forms of mediumship. Occultists have understood these matters for centuries, as many old books will inform us but, as I see it, it is comforting to have them brought into the fresh air of scientific respectability, as long as our white-coated friends are also ready with a few dos and don'ts.

The frontiers of science are expanding so rapidly every day that probably by the time this book is published new facts will have come to light, causing my readers to revise their views and enlarge upon, or discard, what I have suggested. Fair enough, and I shall do likewise. There will be new terms of reference to add to our Aquarian dictionary and, when the next generation comes to learn psychic self-defence, let us hope they will be able to understand the principle and not become bogged down by words.

Alternative therapies are helping to bridge the gap between metaphysical concepts in human psychology and established modes of thinking in psychiatry. Jung expanded on Freud by his consideration of archetypal expression at many levels, thus highlighting the innate need in mankind to search for someone or something beyond his immediate needs. Recent experiments in hypnotherapy have added a new dimension to psychiatry, and a study of the subtle energies that affect the physical and mental health of all life forms on this planet has added credence to many an old and well-established occult teaching.

An open-minded approach is always advisable and students of matters psychic, occult or mystical should make a point of aligning their beliefs with the new discoveries in the scientific field wherever possible. It is my own belief that science will eventually take over many of the fields now exclusively metaphysical, as technology is developed which can establish, measure and correct both physical and mental energy flows at levels not at present deemed feasible.

CHAPTER SEVEN

DREAMS, ASTRAL TRAVEL, AND THE CHAKRAS

Dreams are an important function in the journey of the psyche through the dimensions of inner time, as they act as connecting links between inner and outer time or as lines of communication between the spirit and conscious mind. Dreams function along archetypal lines, so anyone skilled in the interpretation of this symbology can soon unravel what the spirit is trying to convey to the dreamer. But all this is by no means new. All the early races placed great significance on dreams; the Christian Bible, which is the standard book of spiritual reference for so many westerners, abounds with stories of interpreted dreams. Psychiatrists tell us it is good to dream, as dreams act as a sort of safety valve for the emotions and those bottled up frustrations that life so rudely awards us from time to time. It is interesting to note the compensatory aspects of dreams, in that they often depict suffering and worries when the dreamer is not actually going through a bad patch, while those who are having to put up with just about as much as they can take can dream in terms and aspects of beauty and fulfilment.

Can we avoid bad dreams, and what can we do about nightmares? As this book is primarily about psychic self-defence, it is important that we analyse the nature of dreams in this context, so that precautions can be taken to ensure that at least some of the more unpleasant aspects of sleep-time experience can be controlled. Once more we are faced with the question: how many bad dreams are really occult in nature and not simply the result of chemical reactions in our body caused by rich food or alcohol? After all, a very high temperature can cause hallucinations bordering on nightmares, and this is purely a manifestation of a battle taking place in our body between some invading alien body or virus and our own anti-bodies!

What is needed is a logical elimination of all possible NORMAL causes before pinning anything down to the supernatural. If you have retired on a glass of herb tea and a dry biscuit, are in natural good health, have no pressing worries or possible build-up to or symptoms of an oncoming illness, and *then* have a ghastly nightmare, by all means make a metaphysical probe. This particularly applies if you are staying at some unfamiliar place.

One summer I underwent a very frightening experience while staying the night with friends in a very old cottage. I woke up screaming, or so I thought, but it must have been in my sleep as no one else heard a sound. The condition was in the property and not with me, so what did I do? After waking in a state of some agitation I earthed myself thoroughly, rinsed my face and hands in the bathroom next door and drank a glass of clear water, by which time I was in full mental control and able to tackle the matter occultly. I then cleared the atmosphere in the immediate vicinity, banishing unwelcome influences from the room, and called down a protective ray to ensure that the remainder of my night would be peaceful. It was.

Simple procedures for those who know how, you might argue, but in fact I did nothing that anyone reading this book could not do. No ritual was employed, I carried no occult paraphernalia, nor the impedimenta of the magician! Just the creative power of my own mind. Clear water helps to dilute unwanted energies and also acts as a conductor for any forces one might care to invoke in replacement. I visualized my own personal and God symbols, and mentally created a field of light which filled every crack and corner in the room. Through my archetypal symbol I felt the manifested presence of a source of light, guide, angel, call it what you like and, thus protected, I was able to relax into a sound and untroubled sleep.

Persistent nightmares often herald approaching periods of physical illness or mental stress, so care should be taken to observe the omens. For example, to dream continually of eating a particular kind of food which you would not normally consider, could be the subconscious mind's way of telling you that you are missing out some important dietary need. We all have those silly dreams about losing a handbag or wallet, missing a vital train or connection, appearing on stage without knowing our words, or making an unholy mess of a really important job interview. These are purely reflections of the normal stresses of everyday life, our insecurities, suspicions, misjudgments, and so on, and should not be labelled as psychic or occult.

Astral Travel
Let us first of all relate this to the sleep state, or those times when we are in delta brainwaves and fully functioning with REMs (rapid eye movements) or, in occult parlance, well and truly out of the body and away

into some other dimension or time circuit. Is there a form
of protection we can effect when travelling astrally during
sleep state? Of course there is.

Some people are able to programme themselves to
become aware, while in a dream, that they are only
dreaming and act accordingly, rather like Alice in the
children's story realizing that her enemies were 'only a
pack of cards'. In other words, once you can come to
terms with the fact that mental experiences, either in the
sleep state or the waking state, are controllable by mind,
you are half-way there.

A dream where you are being chased by a savage tiger
may fill you with terror but if you can stand still in that
dream and say to yourself, 'Hold on a minute, this tiger is
only a thought-form which I can dissolve by thought
power,' and then try saying 'boo' to it, you'll be surprised
at the wonders it works. Of course this won't act as a
preventive against unwanted out-of-the-body experiences, as one cannot expect the highways and byways of
time to clear automatically at one's approach. But it will
teach you how to cope with, side-step and inhibit, to a
degree, likely encounters of an undesirable or alien
nature.

I'm sure some of my readers will have come across
legends about changing shape or form during unpleasant
astral encounters. Mythology and old occult literature
abound with such tales, one of the best known being in
the Celtic tale of Keridwen and Gwion. Keridwen had a
cauldron of knowledge which she instructed her servant
Gwion to stir for her while she busied herself elsewhere.
During the course of his labours a drop splashed on
Gwion, immediately endowing him with all knowledge.
When Keridwen returned she perceived this, much to her
horror, and realized that the only way to contain this
knowledge was to devour Gwion. But Gwion quickly got
the message and hastily changed form to escape his
pursuer. The story relates how both of them effected
several form changes until finally, in desperation, Gwion
became a grain of corn. Keridwen wisely assumed the

form of a hen and devoured the corn; the law of equalities beautifully illustrated. Yes, it is possible to change form in sleep state, if pursued, and I've frequently done it. How? I can only reply that it's all in the mind!

Of course all astral projection does not take place during the sleep state. The normal sleeping type is labelled 'involuntary'; voluntary astral projection takes place under conscious conditions. Exactly the same precautions apply, although it would appear to be easier to wake up from a difficult involuntary projection than for some people, anyway, to come round after a bad voluntary 'trip'. I have come across many cases where voluntary projection has taken place, under uncontrolled conditions, with disastrous results. Sometimes one is unable to get back into one's body properly, or an auric misalignment occurs which can make one sick or depressed.

A good night's sleep (out of the body again and back in the right way next time) can cure these ills, but there are instances where the aura or the cord can be damaged during an astral affray, and then help is needed either from someone specializing in occult healing or with the right experience. But it is not the end of the world and auric breaches can be repaired, just as accidents to the body can be put right if quickly attended to by a qualified doctor.

If you intend to indulge in lone astral projection experiments, do be *very* careful to take measures for your safety while out of the body. I knew of one case of a gentleman who tried it and couldn't get back. Had it not been for his sister calling in an hour or so later he might have had real problems. Not being into occult interests, she thought he had sustained a stroke and called an ambulance. Medical treatment received at the hospital helped to bring him back but he never tried again and hastily forsook all occult practices from that day on.

Until one is experienced it is advisable *not* to dabble in lone voluntary projection. Work with another, or train properly with an experienced practitioner, either from the field of fringe medicine or the occult, who understands the workings of the subconscious mind and can return you safely to normal in the event of problems arising while you are wandering through uncharted areas of time and space.

Psychic Safety Valves

While dealing with the subject of how the metaphysical world can affect those not necessarily deeply involved, or even making a cursory study of it, a case which I feel is worthy of mention comes to my mind, as it highlights a possible area of danger for the natural psychic who is bordering on mental disorder and shows how those around can watch for and recognize the symptoms. A gentleman I know prided himself on his own clairvoyant abilities, while despising everyone else even vaguely connected with that study. He claimed that he frequently saw 'little people' and also figures standing around in his bedroom. He passed through a period of difficulties with his wife and they eventually separated, but during the period just prior to the separation, when he was feeling particularly bitter, he woke up in the night and 'saw' figures standing over her bed.

On one occasion there was a lady whom he described as the 'Virgin Mary', on another it was St Francis of Assisi and on the third and final occasion, when he was harbouring a particular anger against her as she slept, he was faced with the figure of an Egyptian god-form with an ibis head (Thoth) — to quote his own words — 'whose two beady eyes suddenly met mine with such menace that I was stricken with fear and hastily beat a retreat to my own bed'. He later told his wife about the incident and what had prevented him from giving vent to his anger. She, in turn, related it to her doctor and the doctor explained to her how the mind has its defence mechanisms which come into operation when an emotion contrary to the normal behaviour pattern manifests.

In the doctor's opinion, the figure was a figment of the husband's imagination and acted as a safety valve against his committing an act of violence. 'But,' the doctor cautioned, 'he is obviously near the borderline, and what would happen to you if on one occasion his mind failed to produce such an image. . . .' Needless to say the frightened lady proceeded with her divorce action.

The occultist's answer to all this would naturally be that the wife was protected by archetypal figures, notably Thoth, and had in some former life or time zone rendered good service to the Egyptian god of healing, which merited his protection against mental illness in another. Knowing the lady, I knew this to be the case, but I use this example to illustrate two viewpoints regarding the same phenomenon, i.e. the orthodox medical and the metaphysical.

Chakras

It would not be in order to tackle the subject of psychic self-defence without explaining the functions of the chakric system and therefore the dangers to be encountered from its misuse.

The word 'chakra' is said by some to mean 'wheel' while I have also heard it translated as 'spinning knife'. What, in fact, we are dealing with is vortices of energy, or a series of small force fields which act as inter-connecting links between the subtler frequencies imperceptible to the five senses and the physical body. There are seven chakras relating to the human body, although I have information concerning a possible eighth not normally used or even acknowledged in many occult schools.

Each chakra equates with an area of the human anatomy and one of the endocrine glands. Imbalances in the energy flow between the chakra and its related endocrine gland can cause imbalances and illness involving the organ or organs concerned. The *kundalini*, or serpent fire, so often talked about in eastern mysticism, is a spiral force which is said to lie dormant at the base of the spine in the region of the lower, or *muladhara*, chakra until it is awakened by spiritual seeking, when it begins to uncoil in serpent fashion and ascend the spinal column, touching off the other chakras as it goes. With the awakening of each chakra, subtle changes are said to take place in the personality and, unless this development is carefully balanced, psychic problems can definitely occur for the student.

There are several schools of thought regarding the *kundalini*: some occultists consider it in terms of an ascending level of consciousness which can be controlled by physical and mental disciplines such as meditation and yoga, while others opine that its ascent is more a question of spiritual growth and evolution as related to the age of the soul. Opinions also vary regarding the nature of each chakra and endocrine gland, so the list I shall give will be a general one and not related to any particular doctrinal belief or school of magic.

Chakra	Endocrine Gland	Area of the Body
muladhara	gonads	base of spine
svadisthana	pancreas	sacral
manipura	adrenals	solar plexus
anahata	thymus	breasts/heart
visuddhu	thyroid/para-thyroid	throat
ajna	pineal	between the eyes
sahasrara	pituitary	top of head

Many occult healers work through the chakras because, as I have already explained, it is possible for the energy flow to become out of alignment, bringing on a complaint associated with the related endocrine gland or body area. For example, a blockage in the area of the *muladhara* chakra, which governs the reproductory organs and sex functions, can cause either a mental hang-up about sex or difficulties of a physical nature within the organs themselves. The skilled occult healer can unblock and re-align the chakric channels so that the force flows freely through them. Perhaps it is the *visuddhu* chakra which has become out of alignment with the throat area and the person experiences frequent throat troubles or difficulty in expressing himself vocally; likewise a blockage at the *ajna* centre could cause distorted clairvoyance, headaches, migraines and a sense of disorientation. Chakric weaknesses show up clearly in a horoscope, as students of medical astrology will know.

It is not advisable to experiment with chakric healing unless one knows what one is doing. Believe it or not, the will to heal and good healing intentions are not enough to effect a healing, especially if one is dealing with forces one does not understand. As many budding exorcists have discovered to their chagrin, all is not cut and dried or black and white when it comes to the human mind and it is no use chanting away 'devils' when the poor sufferer has a physical brain tumour or a virus infection. Leave chakric problems to those who *really* know about them and don't be taken in my somebody who says they have read a few books.

CHAPTER EIGHT

PSYCHIC WORK IN PRACTICE

What is termed the 'fireside occultist' can often present a problem for the genuine practitioner. As with everything else in life, one can only learn so much theory, the rest is all practice and is only perfected in the school of life. After all, you would not think of performing a surgical operation to remove an appendix after reading how to do it a few times in a medical book. In medical school you would observe the action in progress and finally be allowed to take the knife under the watchful gaze and practised hand of a senior surgeon. So why not apply rules of that sort to matters psychic and occult?

Metaphysical book knowledge makes for a good conversation piece in certain company and, if you can quote from this or that in an erudite manner, there are bound to be those present who are uninformed themselves and therefore easily impressed. In fact, you might even be approached for an opinion, a psychic 'look in', or to do a nice juicy exorcism job! If you are more prudent than proud you will pass the matter off with 'well, I've only read about these things, of course, I've never actually practised them', but ego trippers could well see some imagined glory for themselves and have a go, producing disastrous results for all parties concerned and creating a karmic debt to boot.

One cannot learn about the psychic or occult simply from reading books; it has to be experienced to be understood. If you want to stay cosily in your armchair reading your ghost stories, Satanic novels or Qabalistic rituals, keep it that way and replace your book on its shelf when you have finished; but, should you feel prompted to delve further and involve yourself in some practical application of your studies, proceed with caution.

Psychic Work Proper

I shall now come to that part of my book which is specially for those who have chosen the path, be it as a medium, mystic or occultist. So let us first of all consider the medium who is working in the field, or students who have taken their first steps in the practice of their art for the benefit of the public (or their private bank account, as the case may be).

Mr Smith needs help and advice, so he searches the pages of his 'local' and there, lo and behold, he sees an advertisement which reads 'Clara Field, crystal reader and clairvoyant, bring your problems to me', and so on. Just the person, he thinks, so after a telephone booking he trots happily off to consult the lady.

Now Mr Smith has one particular problem. He is employed by a firm that is rapidly expanding its business abroad; he doesn't stand much chance of making it into management in England, because those above him are still young and he is not all that well qualified. But his superiors have offered him promotion if he is prepared to move to Brazil in the autumn. Mr Smith has a small semi-detached in the suburbs, a wife who does part-time work at the local telephone exchange and a nine-year-old boy at a small private school. He knows his wife won't want to go abroad as her mother lives nearby and his son is doing well in the school football team. But secretly he visualizes himself sitting in a spacious white office with the tropical sun streaming through the windows and an army of cheap labour at his beck and call. He has, in fact, thought of nothing but this for some days prior to contacting the clairvoyant.

Mr Smith arrives at the consulting rooms and the lady takes a look at her crystal ball. 'I see a foreign land, a large room with white walls; sir, you are about to go abroad.' Madame Field has simply telepathized with Mr Smith and relayed back to him his own visualization. When he proceeds to tell her about his wife and son she shrugs it off by replying, 'You are destined to go there because I see you there.' And so the man goes on his way, still totally unsure. Either way he can be caught. If he doesn't take the opportunity offered he may feel cheated, and a slow resentment could build up that will eventually lead to the break-up of his marriage. Or, if he goes abroad, he could risk losing his wife that way. Decisions, decisions, as the saying goes.

What I am trying to illustrate here is that ultimately we must be responsible for fashioning our own life. A good clairvoyant can help by giving us hope in dark days and, of course, there ARE instances where the medium is time-projecting and not simply telepathizing. But in cases of straight clairvoyance these instances are, in my opinion, rare and, until the aspiring psychic has a bit of counselling experience under his belt, it can be very much a hit-and-miss affair.

Psychic Aids

This leads me to time symbols, the name I have coined for divinatory aids such as the tarot, runes, *I Ching*, and so on. Here we have rather a different kettle of fish, where the conscious mind is cut out to a degree, although even then, when it comes to interpretation, there can be prejudice. I recall an instance of a lady who was almost into middle age but desperately wanted a second child. Her only son had been born to her in an unhappy marriage when she was eighteen, and she had since made a very good second match, which had not been blessed with progeny. She visited a series of mediums and asked the obvious question. Each, in turn, enquired how old she was. When she mentioned being in her mid-forties they shook their heads sadly and advised her to take up other interests; they said this regardless of what tarot cards came up or what appeared active in her horoscope. Actually she had the last laugh on them and produced a child, but the lesson to be learned from this is never to interpret in terms of what *you* think, or what convention or prevailing custom might decree.

People are individuals. Tarot readers who see a card indicating that the enquirer might have, say, a great writing talent but, because they see a mousy little housewife, change the meaning of the card as the concept strains their credulity, are bad psychics. In other words, folks, defend yourself against YOURSELF when you are giving a service to the public. Subjectivity is just as valid an obstacle to truth as is the mischievous elementary spirit who misleads for fun.

One can only learn so much from a textbook about any psychic aid; after that it is up to the aspirant's skill and feeling for psychology as to whether he or she develops into a talented delineator.

Defence During Readings

A lady I knew who practised as a clairvoyant in central London frequently complained that certain visitors brought with them bad vibes that upset her and left a nasty atmosphere in her rooms. By the law of averages there are bound to be people one meets in life whose vibes jar with one's own. One cannot be compatible with everyone, even if similar views and beliefs are shared. I am often asked by non-believers why it is that there are so many different viewpoints among occultists and psychics;

surely if there were one truth, some must be right and others wrong.

Of course there is no 'one truth' in the metaphysical field, just as there is no one truth in Christianity, Buddhism or any other 'ism'. An idea is cast forth, and people interpret it according to their own stage of spiritual development on the one hand and environmental programming on the other. Only the really 'old souls' are able to rise above dogma and tribalism and relate to the universe as a whole. So the world of the occult is the same as everything else in this respect. Views will and do differ and there is no absolute. The sooner this is realized and applied to all things in life, the sooner this planet will become a more harmonious place in which to live and work out one's karma.

In view of the likelihood of coming across people and/or discarnate entities or cosmic energies that are inharmonious or even in opposition to one's own, are there any precautions one can take to keep out of a 'clash' situation? There are indeed, but it takes a cool head to carry them through when some one or some thing is proving particularly niggling. If you find yourself in a position in life where you have need to serve the public in some psychic form, here are a few tips for 'safety first'.

Always ensure that any room you work in is kept as clean as possible at the physical/material level. Dirt attracts the lower astral and it's no use sweeping it under the carpet and hoping the spirits won't see it. Remember, they have etheric sight if you haven't! Like attracts like. Cleanliness attracts cleanliness. A clean mind attracts other clean minds. Sincerity draws sincere thoughts towards you. As ye sow so shall ye reap and all that. So ensure that you are clean in body, mind and surroundings to start with.

Next you must build a good psychic atmosphere. Depending upon your persuasion, draw light into your room. If you are a Christian you might feel happy with a prayer before you start work, a cross on the wall or a reading from scripture. A Buddhist might go for a meditation, incense and a small shrine. A Pantheist would feel safe with the symbols of the four elements, a Qabalist with the Tree of Life and so forth. The psychic working as a lone consultant MUST learn to detach himself both psychically and emotionally from his enquirers. Be sympathetic but don't allow your caller to overpower your sentiments, and the same goes for those who try to force their wills over yours. And you *will* meet them!

I worked for many years with an occult healing group and we had a gentleman with us who worked as a trance medium. He would occasionally undertake public work but when he did we always ensured that he was 'covered' by an occultist. This covering consisted of projecting a strong thought force around him which was attached to the coverer, so that any intruding mind or influence encountered a kind of 'force field' and, if there were any malignant intentions, it was the coverer and not the medium who drew them off.

Our coverers used to place this protection around the medium before he entered the trance state and, when the entity wishing to communicate made its presence felt, it would immediately make contact with the force field. It was then the duty of the coverer to issue the law of challenge, to ensure that the communicator was of light and not a 'nasty' or mischief maker on the loose. According to the law of challenge, if the coverer is of lesser power than the entity, the latter will get in anyway but, if it be of lesser power than the coverer, then it must await the coverer's 'all clear' to take over the medium. Of course, a being of light more powerful than the coverer would simply reply with a recognizable signal and pass through the cover harmoniously.

I recall with horror how one medium, not of our group, told me how she had been sitting in a session where another was in trance, supposedly 'taking' the group, when a terrible entity took over the medium, who spat and uttered curses while frothing at the mouth, and so on. In the school of occult discipline in which I trained, NO ENTITY OF THIS NATURE WOULD HAVE BEEN ALLOWED IN THE ROOM, LET ALONE PERMITTED TO ACTUALLY TAKE OVER A MEDIUM UNDER OUR CARE AND PROTECTION.

So, if any of you are sitting with a medium who enters the trance state and you sense an atmosphere that feels uncomfortable, or the medium starts to show signs of distress or alienation, bring them round immediately and clear the room, either by the use of thought power or via prayer or ritual if you are of that bent. Banishing rituals are plentiful and any good book on the subject will provide you with many to choose from. Personally I find it simpler to use mind power to create barriers of resistance against unwanted intelligences or unbridled energies but, of course, it is better in the first place not to invoke that which you cannot handle; I shall deal with this subject in more detail under a later heading.

CHAPTER NINE

THE REINCARNATION QUESTION

It is not uncommon to find the psychic faculty starting to develop or blossom forth after a few sessions of deep hypnosis. One gentleman I know who had recourse to hypnotism for persistent migraine ended up as a trance medium.

Those who find the normal processes of psychic development difficult to master may cope better with the faculty with the help of a hypnotist. But not everyone is a good hypnotic subject, just as not all of us are potentially good psychics. So why are some people born 'knowing' or, to use occult terminology, are 'old souls', while others appear to be unable to extricate themselves from certain set grooves of existence or mundane thinking patterns?

Before resorting to reincarnation as the only answer, it is wise to explore alternative concepts. After all, there are many people who are misled into believing themselves to be something they are not simply by ego-tripping into other time zones, and this in itself constitutes a danger to happiness and balanced living. For instance, how about cases when more than one person feels an affinity with some name from the past? I have met several perfectly honest and genuine psychics who have each claimed to be the reincarnation of the Pharaoh Akhnaton. If the 'one soul per life' theory is correct someone must be mistaken, so what must we learn from this?

One theory is that of the 'collective unconscious' as defined by Jung. In other words, we do not experience different lives in other time zones or periods of history, but only once, in the 'now'. But, if we are able to open up our subconscious minds to the ocean of cosmic consciousness, either through a disciplined path such as meditation or mystical studies, or through natural abilities, we can then become any person we wish, simply by tuning in to the experiences of that personality.

A very dear friend of mine, who is both a medium and scientifically oriented, gave the following analogy which could also serve as an explanation as to why some people are born 'aware' and others appear to pass through life blinkered:

'When we are born into the physical world each of us is allotted a special frequency with which we may tune in to the cosmic unconscious. When we turn on our radios we scan the frequency spectrum until we find a station we like, and we may choose to stay with that station and listen to no other. But a radio station does not play the same programme over and over; it provides a variety of entertainment. At one time we may tune into a news broadcast; or a symphony; or a play; or a sporting event. All of these may be on the same frequency or station, but each has its own time slot. Perhaps we can be likened to that radio receiver, picking up those cosmic programmes and reports to which we have a special affinity, compatibility or frequency. But, unfortunately, most of our radio receivers are not properly attuned and we hear only an intelligible voice breaking briefly through the static which drowns out most of our programmes. Most people experience an occasional flash of psychic awareness and a few will recognize them as such. More unfortunate, however, are those people whose receivers are not turned on at all, for they drift through life in total silence wondering. . . .'

Rather well put, I thought, and so easy to apply to people we may all know in the world around us.

A few years ago I undertook to research the 'past lives' phenomenon and carried out some experiments with people I did not know at all. One interesting coincidence that cropped up time and time again was the accent on one or other archetype which seemed to follow through a series of lives. Let me illustrate: a gentleman wrote to me for impressions of his former lives. He signed himself plain 'Mr' and the address was a normal one. Using psychometry and his letter I received a set of clairvoyant impressions all of which were associated with military set-ups in the past. There was a soldier who marched behind Rameses; a lady Alexandrian camp follower; a Roman legionary; a Crusader on horseback; and so forth right up to the 1914-18 war. All very strange, thought I, but I felt honour bound to relay what I had seen. A few days later I received a 'thank-you' letter from 'Sgt ...., Catterick Camp'. If my friend's analogy is correct, I had simply tuned in to the sergeant's wavelength and was picking up his programme. Perhaps he had actually lived those lives, or perhaps they were being experienced simultaneously in parallel universes or time zones by other members of his group soul or martial archetype?

I have, in fact, found it dangerous to investigate former lives, or supposed former lives, without considering the subject of time and all that it implies. I can accept that the spirit has a basic archetypal nature which it expresses in many time zones, but whether these are actual individual lives or simply group soul experiences that can be tuned into, is a debatable point.

I am personally of the opinion that past lives are not always as many as psychics or occultists envisage them. For example, I do not see time as linear, but curving, and it is possible to move through it, backward and forward. Therefore, those who can move ahead in it would gain more knowledge and earn the label 'old soul'. Hypnosis lends credence to this theory, as one can be regressed or progressed. I have first-hand experience of this and it has shown me that in both progression and regression the subconscious mind relays its information symbolically. Like psychism, progressive hypnotherapy has its pitfalls, because the subconscious mind would only appear to release such information regarding the future as it deems necessary to help combat the stress of the present. Names, dates, descriptions tend to be more symbolic than precise so, as with ESP, it is very much a question of decoding those symbols, which requires a degree of skill.

Experience has tended to indicate to me that reincarnation, in the general linear-time accepted mode, is not a valid truth, and I am more inclined to the belief that the answer to the riddle of the evolving soul and its 'memories' of former lives is tied up with time. There would seem to be an outer time point where all time zones converge, an 'eternal now'. This can be approached through a series of steps or plateaux, each of which affords the out-of-the-body viewer an ever widening concept of the universe and an ever deepening insight into his own mind and the minds of others. No doubt we have been, or are, some of the things we remember, but simultaneously, as though our spirits are fragmented into different time zones, all of which are happening at once. Many instances of 'recollection' are, as I see it, tune-ins to other members of the group soul, or simply probes into the great universal unconscious.

The ego or spirit expresses its basic archetypal nature in any situation or period of time appropriate to the experience it requires to afford it the understanding necessary to return to the Centre Point, All Time, God, call it what you will. Tradition expresses this principle in terms of linear time, but I postulate that the Aquarian Age will bring down the barriers of time and space and present old truths in a new, more scientific light. All these points are debatable and I am simply presenting them as considerations and not *ex cathedra*, so the question is purely academic. But, as there are so many anomalies when it comes to the reincarnation question, it is advisable to keep an open mind or one's faith could be shattered or one's credulity so strained as to turn one off any arcane teachings. As the guide of my dear friend said to me, 'One man's truth is another man's folly.'

There is a constancy in the soul nature that would appear to run through all life patterns, which does not, however, deny experiences outside the archetype but rather inclines it towards a form of expression sympathetic or complementary to, if not actually of, the soul group principle. Applying all this to matters psychic or occult will give a fairly clear idea as to who is drawn to the 'path' and who is not. It may be argued that everyone is psychic to a greater or lesser degree, which is true in one sense. But then there are many who can sing or dance who are not destined to become public performers, so it is a question of getting one's gifts into perspective. To overreach oneself in psychic matters can have disastrous results but, equally, one should not bury one's talent.

Those psychics to whom the procedure and practice of their art come naturally have obviously travelled that road in other time zones or, to use more orthodox terms, they have the right karmic past. Some are born knowing and automatically erect all the necessary safety precautions as a matter of normal logic. Sometimes they borrow from the religions they have been raised in; at other times the symbology employed or *modus operandi* simply comes from within and can be attributed to external schooling, i.e. via the group soul or time travel. The experienced psychic, like the experienced traveller, knows how to read the signposts, where to catch the right connections, what to do if the lights go out while passing through a tunnel, and at which station or shore to disembark.

Newcomers to the scene, to whom this type of information does not come naturally, should ensure that safety first disciplines are carefully observed EVERY TIME and on EVERY PSYCHIC OCCASION or voyage into outer time. Anyone ignoring the highway code of the cosmos will meet with problems of one kind or another sooner or later, and ignorance of the law is no excuse. The universe is NOT anarchistic by nature, much as the less disciplined among us would like to believe that it is. I once heard the age of the soul defined thus: the young soul says 'I know', the middle-aged soul says 'I think I know' and the old soul says 'I don't know'. Think about it!

CHAPTER TEN

THE LODGE SYSTEM

For the remainder of this book I shall concentrate upon the dangers likely to be encountered in the pursuit of the path and much of what I say may sound bizarre to the layman.

As already explained, it is NOT advisable to mix rays, systems, schools, and so on. Stay with one until you have mastered it and know what you are doing. Not all occult systems or traditions are compatible one with another and there are also rays that can cancel each other out, which many students do not realize. For example, the ray in any system which relates to the Saturnian principle is the natural anti-ray to the Uranian principle. These principles are re-echoed in all that comes under their rulership. The planetary metal of Saturn is lead and of Uranus, uranium. Uranium in its radioactive form is encased in lead for protection and, in just the same way, an invocation to the Uranian principle can be held back or cancelled out by invoking the Saturnian principle.

The easy way to recognize rays and anti-rays is to understand the principles which each represent for, remember, all archetypes are constant in all systems. Thus a Pan ray that is earthy and of a 'quickening' nature can be countered by a Neptunian ray that diffuses, disperses and distracts. I have worked with these principles myself and had ample evidence of their efficacy. On one occasion I was asked to send some occult help to quell a particularly violent riot. We used a Neptunian-type ray with immediate success. The rioters started to look around, their attention suddenly distracted by someone playing a guitar at the back of the crowd. Slowly the music took over and their interest was completely diverted. It was quite incredible to watch on a TV set!

Equally, rays of an expanding nature such as Jupiter/Chesed/Thor, and so on, depending on which system you are working in, can be countered by a ray that destroys, changes, throws out the old and established and brings in the new, such as Pluto/Anubis/Aurochs. So, if you are a beginner, do check that your work isn't partially or wholly cancelling itself out and, if you feel pressurized by others, negate that pressure with an appropriate anti-ray rather than trying to fight back. One should never embark upon deliberate occult battle. Defence is permitted by cosmic law, but these laws do NOT condone the old military idea that attack is the best method of defence.

Occult Ranks
Too much nonsense has been talked about dubious occult titles and what they represent and there are even those gullible enough to believe that, if they pay a handsome fee to this or that organization, they will receive in exchange the wisdom of the universe plus a £5 scroll telling them that they are an adeptus major or even an ipsissimus! Occult expertise CANNOT BE BOUGHT, nor can it be taught, if the aspirant does not possess the

soul age or soul quality necessary for the path. Sitting a series of mocked up examination papers that require one to know the layout of this or that ritual is NO GUIDE to true wisdom. Wisdom and knowledge are NOT synonymous, although it does help an aspiring occultist or magician if they are born with a horoscope revealing a degree of intellectuality or the ability to translate esoteric knowledge and experiences, for which there are no terms of reference, into language understandable to the man in the street or the persons they have incarnated to teach or help.

It is of little use ascending to great mystical heights if that experience is purely selfish and does not relate to the era or time zone into which one has incarnated. The truly great masters or old souls are able to convey the deepest and most abstract concept in terms easily comprehensible to younger souls. 'Unless ye become as little children. . .' and so forth. So avoid intellectual athletics and keep to simple, uncomplicated principles which can be applied at any level in life or, if necessary, to the timeless world of the abstract.

Set ranks such as those used in the famous Order of the Golden Dawn are not reliable guides to either occult prowess or wisdom. Many lodges do have their own individually tailored ranking systems, but because one has risen to the rank of, say, imperator in one order does not mean that one is automatically at the same level of development as someone with a similarly named rank in another lodge. Better, by far, to be yourself and not try for fancy diplomas, because in the final analysis nobody is going to give you a spiritual honours degree in wisdom. The universe simply does not function that way.

Secret Temple Training

The lodge system dates back to ancient times, when certain sections of temple training were considered unsuitable for everyone and, therefore, were kept secret. Following the advent of Christianity, when it became unsafe to pursue arcane practices openly for fear of persecution or inquisition, those wishing to carry out occult work were obliged to do so in secret in fear for their lives and those of their families. Over a period of many years, hidden or secret orders flourished, although not all of those that history has labelled 'occult' were in fact so and many a political intrigue was hatched within the *sanctum sanctorum* of some supposed magical sect.

We do not have space here to indulge in a history of secret orders, but one of the most famous and most suspect of the many that mushroomed in the eighteenth century was the Illuminati. Under the leadership of one Adam Weishaupt, a whole network of questionable pursuits was practised and, in order to raise funds for his nefarious schemes, Weishaupt instituted a special 'rank', within his lodge system, that endowed the privileged student with the title of 'Scottish knight'. This rank was reserved for those who were materially rich but psychically or occultly useless and, needless to say, a lot of flattery went with it. As each 'Scottish knight' was sworn to secrecy upon initiation, every man believed himself to be the only one so favoured and contributed generously in appreciation of being held in such exalted spiritual esteem! Echoed today, methinks, in the advertisements selling instant wisdom for a fat fee.

There are lodges in existence within the many systems and traditions but these are seldom as visualized by romantics. It is difficult to run a good lodge successfully in this day and age, because of the pressures of everyday living and the fact that most people work in some way and cannot devote as much time to occult practices as could those of the privileged classes a century or so ago. Petty jealousies often flourish within lodges and this bears out the old occult saying that is re-echoed in the scriptures: to ruin or break a lodge the best aimed blows are from within, as in the Bible, where the strong man or head of the household must of necessity be bound before his domains can be taken over. Evil forces working either from other dimensions, or via the suspect intentions of rival practitioners, can best destroy the good work done by a lodge by infiltrating it and causing disharmony or havoc amongst its members. This does actually happen and your writer has first-hand experience of it.

So, to avoid dangers of this kind or to defend yourself occultly against unwelcome vibes, make sure that those people you invite to join your lodge are either on the same ray as yourselves and not strongly associated with an anti-ray; or have your scryer take a look into their evolutionary past or cosmic origins to see where they learned their trade. Those who were originally instructed in the temples of Heliopolis, for example, would not find it easy to work harmoniously with anyone trained in the Hebrew tradition. Only with old souls, who have risen above all earth systems and attained to a degree of cosmic consciousness, will a harmony be achieved in spite of past karmic links.

Any lodge that is run along correct and disciplined lines will function satisfactorily as long as its members' vibes are harmonious one with another. Jealousy, resentment, ego-tripping, power seeking and the like constitute an Open Sesame to malign influences for, remember, evil cannot exist if it is not nurtured and regularly fed. If a group of persons, all possessing powerful personalities in their own right, try to work together, it is more than likely that there will sooner or later be a clash of wills. The genuine old soul knows how to subjugate his ego for the good of the whole. Only young souls seek to promote their personalities at the expense of harmony. The old soul has seen all the ego tripping before and worked through it, he no longer needs to prove anything, either to himself or others, so if and when evil attacks through the door of pride he quietly exits and leaves the laws of karma to deal with the situation.

There is much talk, most of it idle, about such things as special lodge handshakes, calling codes, and so on. Many nineteenth century orders did have private signals of this sort, originally to avoid persecution, and some Masonic institutions have perpetuated this practice to the present day. Significant handshakes are also used in Wicca and amongst Pantheistic groups, although their original significance has become obscured, rather like those stories passed around at parties which end up very garbled. Regarding 'calling codes', I have employed one of these myself and during a period of stress and attack had recourse to it with amazing results. My SOS was most certainly picked up, but not at all by the person or persons I might have imagined.

Working the Egyptian system at the time, I found my greatest response and support came from Wicca and Pantheistic groups, which taught me something important about ray affinities. I have not found the Christian tradition to be very compatible with the Egyptian, although history informs us that much of Essenism seeped through from the Nile region, whereas Norse magic certainly does not quarrel with its Egyptian cousin, in spite of the distance between the countries of origin.

Qabalistic lodges appear to be compatible with Christian tradition, which is logical if you think about it, but eastern and western magical codes are not always easy to match so, would-be lodge leaders, try to avoid mixing oil and water and you'll find it easier to steer a safe course through the troubled waters of the earthly ego.

CHAPTER ELEVEN

ELEMENTALS AND THOUGHT-FORMS

There is some confusion of terms where elementals and elementary spirits are concerned. In my terms of reference, an elementary spirit is a lesser evolved entity, probably from the sphere of pre-human existence or some other time zone that has not yet offered it the opportunity to advance its evolution. Some occultists employ this term when describing thought-forms generated by the use of magical invocations plus will, but I am not one of them.

In my understanding, elementals are spirits of the four elements, fire, air, water and earth. These I categorize under the heading of the deva kingdoms, as I was taught (and still believe) that they evolve through a series of experiences unique to their own kind, eventually gaining their fourfold nature and ascending to the angelic kingdoms. The spirits of fire were named salamanders by the ancients; those of the air were named sylphs; those of water, ondines and those of earth, gnomes.

Specific qualities in human terms are ascribed to each element. The salamanders are associated with creativity, ardour, raw energy, valour and loyalty; the sylphs with intellectuality, speed, communication, detachment and inventiveness; the ondines with the emotions, feelings, receptivity, understanding and sympathy; and the gnomes with thrift, acquisition, wealth in all forms, conservation and practicality. The four 'humours' or psychological types as outlined by Hippocrates are also associated with the elements thus: fire — the sanguine; air — the bilious; water — the phlegmatic; earth — the melancholic.

The spirits of the elements are a vital key in occult development, not only because it is part and parcel of ritualistic procedure to invoke them, but because to conquer the human traits associated with each element is what initiation is all about. As we are all individuals, one or other element will be predominant in our psychological make-up. We may be intense, loyal and creative like the salamanders, or practical and careful like the gnomes. Whichever elemental quality is strongest and most secure in our character will be the deciding factor as to which elemental chooses to escort us along the path of magic, for if the occultist is worth his or her salt this will surely happen.

It was taught in olden times, and is still believed by many today, that when the old soul steps on to the path, his first companion is an elemental spirit who will voluntarily guard him and aid him in his work and studies. I have found this to be absolutely true, although I make no claims to being 'old' or 'wise'. My own first companion was a salamander, who once saved me from what could have been a vicious *physical* attack while travelling.

As one develops and comes to terms with those traits in oneself which are relevant to each element, so one is said to gain one's fourfold nature, after which no further incarnations in dense matter are necessary, other than in a teaching capacity.

Just as there are positive traits associated with each element, so are there also negative aspects. Negative salamander energies are destructive, bossy, cowardly and disloyal; negative sylph energies are pseudo-intellectual, cunning, cruel and unstable; negative ondine energies are misused sexuality, deviousness, selfishness and false psychism; and negative gnome energies are miserliness, dourness, parsimony and love of wealth for its own sake. Obviously there are many variations on each theme but the principles are the same.

Some magicians believe in invoking elementals to do their bidding BEFORE they have mastered the principles of the element in question. This will always cause trouble, as elementals do not care to serve those whom they despise as not having attained to a mastery over their kingdoms by initiatory means, either in the school of life or through occult disciplines. It is NOT always necessary to pass through a series of mystical ascensions to attain to elemental qualities. Such achievement can be just as easily won in any field of human endeavour which contributes in some just way to the cause of cosmic law or the broadening of spiritual understanding on this planet (or any other time zone or planet, as the case may be).

So, student occultist, if you wish to play safe and avoid repercussions, do NOT act in a high-handed manner towards your elemental brothers, or sooner or later the tide will turn and you will wonder what hit you. The spirits of the elements are best won by love, friendship and acknowledgment. If they do choose to help you, thank them. Nothing in the universe should ever be taken for granted. Believe it or not, good manners were not the exclusive prerogative of Victorian times, any more than love, sympathy and understanding belong to any special period of earth history. These are cosmic references and part and parcel of cosmic law.

When I was working with a well-known occult group, I never ceased to be amazed at how many people who termed themselves 'spiritual' lacked the common courtesy to acknowledge a letter, donation, session of free healing or the caring work of genuine souls. Spirituality at one level only, i.e. showing off with a display of 'holier than thou' attitudes, strange apparel, and so on, is a false flag to serve under and will sooner or later fall apart as it lacks the firm foundation of love, warmth and understanding. So, dear student, if you wish to avoid the downward spiral of egoism and its accompanying influences, put yourself in the shoes of others and think how YOU would feel if treated in that way. As the Red Indians so wisely say, 'How can you tell the pain in your brother's foot unless you wear his moccasin?'

Thought-Forms

What exactly is a thought-form? It is basically a pocket of ensouled energy. The alchemists of old used to work at creating an *homunculus* or artificial humanoid, which they hoped to ensoul in some way and thus master the power of creation. Not dissimilar to modern experiments in genetics, except that the scientists seem happy to let in whatever wants to enter, as they do not necessarily acknowledge that all life forms are accompanied by a thought-propulsion unit that we esotericists (and many religious folk) call a spirit.

But occultists are not normally involved in genetic engineering, cloning or similar somatic feats; the thought-forms associated with psychic phenomena are usually pockets of energy endowed with a degree of intelligence, or the qualities of an individual entity, by the originator. Cosmic energy can be summoned by ritual or thought-power, as I have previously described. The operator can then direct this energy so that it behaves in a fashion akin to human behaviour. Thought-forms can be manifested either intentionally or accidentally. In the second instance they can result from negative energies such as frustration, hatred, jealousy or the desire to destroy.

Let us take an example. Miss Smith is sitting with a psychic group that has attracted a degree of cosmic energy as a result of its work. Now Miss Smith falls in love with Mr Brown in the same group, but Mr Brown's preference is for Mrs Jones, also in the group. Miss Smith tries hard to bury her disappointment, but during one particular session, when the power is running high, her feelings get the better of her and she gives vent to thoughts of hatred and negativity against Mrs Jones. Those thoughts are so strong that they infest the power present and the whole thing attaches itself to Mrs Jones. Thus an artificial elemental or thought-form has been accidentally created.

Mrs Jones may start to feel discomfort. Perhaps her health will deteriorate, or bad luck will crop up in her everyday dealings. Unless someone in that group wakes up to the presence of Miss Smith's thought-form and dissolves it, there will be problems all round. You see, the thought-form has to feed on something, so it draws from its originator, Miss Smith, who also starts to feel the strain. Equally it may draw from the group workings, rocking the boat for everyone and probably causing the group to break up, each member slowly becoming dissatisfied, jealous or niggly about some minor matter.

So how would a group leader handle the situation? Bear in mind that it is thought from Miss Smith, plus a pocket of cosmic energy, that is creating the miscreant, so obviously it must be tackled at its own level: by the power of thought and in accordance with the law of equalities. Let us assume that by this occult law the group leader is more powerful occultly than Miss Smith. He will dissolve her thought-form by dismissing the energy to its source of origin (in my early days of study this used to be referred to as sending things back to their rightful sphere of activity or evolution), and rebounding Miss Smith's original negative thought back to Miss Smith. The latter must be undertaken with care, so that it is re-absorbed into her aura as a lesson and not simply catapulted back at her, as that could have the effect of an auric shock. All a matter of occult healing, really.

Having dealt with the procedure for dismissing or dissolving an unwanted thought-form, how would one go about creating one? My immediate advice would be 'don't, there's no reason whatsoever to do so'. But there are occultists who believe in this practice, so if you insist on crossing that road you might as well learn how to heed the oncoming traffic. Some perfectly ethical magicians invoke energies or forces and ensoul them with a thought-beingness with the idea of protecting a loved one, property, places sacred to their gods and so forth. The ancient Egyptians were great ones for this, as may be evidenced in the repercussions suffered by those impious persons who dared to violate certain tombs. The Egyptian priests of old favoured the use of elemental spirits for this purpose, particularly fire, which is why so many molesters of sacred Egyptian places met with fiery ends or violent accidents. But there were those who employed thought-forms or 'artificial elementals', in which context I am not referring to the spirits of the elements.

The *modus operandi* for creating and ensouling thought-forms simply involves attracting or generating subtle energies which are then fashioned into entity form and endowed with individual qualities, usually an essence of the magician; or, alternatively, encouraging some other discarnate spirit or alien intelligence to utilize the power on a temporary basis. In my humble opinion this is a dangerous practice and an entirely unnecessary one. Protections can be effected by magical means without having recourse to such measures. Besides, once activated, these entities can be difficult to dissolve if their originator dies or loses contact and can, therefore, prove something of a problem. In all occult working the law of equalities operates, so it would need an occultist of equal power, or more powerful than the originator, to dismiss the unwanted 'guest' and restore the *status quo*.

As time does not exist in the next dimension in the same way that it does here, a thought-form, once created, can exist for centuries in earth time and be a thorough nuisance until some powerful practitioner comes face to face with it and releases it. These last remarks apply, of course, to the encapsulation of an actual spirit within a falsely created energy field and not necessarily to a thought-form that has been generated simply by someone thinking a life into it from their own personal psyche. The old Arabian stories of genii imprisoned in bottles are true and are actually folk memories of a knowledge possessed by the Egyptians centuries ago. The grateful genie, once released from the bottle, would grant favours to the person kind enough to give it freedom and this, too, is true. I have personally released a trapped elemental (spirit of the elements and not an artificial thought-form) and received much help and affection from it.

The Egyptians favoured salamanders, as I have already mentioned, and in the Arabian stories the released genie was inevitably a djinn. In occult lore 'Djinn' was the name given to the king of the fire elementals who resided in the igneous regions, according to the Abbé de Villars and other 17th- and 18th-century writers on the subject. So, rather than play about trying to create false cosmic impressions, it is better to ask the elemental spirits direct for protection. If the request is made with love and sincerity it will be answered and no ensouling process is necessary or ethically correct, in my view.

How to Inhibit Phenomena
I am often asked how one can stop something frightening from manifesting when one would rather that it didn't! Which reminds me of an amusing story of a lady medium

I knew some years ago, who did a lot of public work but more on an inspirational than a phenomenal level. One night, she told me, while undressing for bed she became aware of a tremendous psychic force building up in her wardrobe. She became convinced that a materialization of some kind was about to occur and that she had only to open her wardrobe to behold . . . what . . . ? 'Whatever did you do?' I enquired curiously. She hesitated in an embarrassed fashion before replying, 'I dived into bed, put my head under the bedclothes in terror and asked it to go away. . . .'

This reaction must be typical of so many of us who may be convinced of the existence of intelligent thought or spirit life after death, or the existence of such entities without a physical vehicle, but who fear actually being brought face to face with the idea. I can't say I go a bundle on spooky visitations myself. In fact, on one occasion I was invited to stay at a stately home in the north which was reputedly VERY haunted. Upon arrival fairly late in the evening I was informed that my host and hostess had been unavoidably delayed until the following day, but an elderly servant would make me comfortable in the west wing and return in the morning to prepare my breakfast.

As I was led up the sweeping staircase and along what seemed to be a never-ending passage, I became aware of spirit eyes watching me. I was shown to my room, an enormous but beautifully appointed suite, and was bidden goodnight. The adjoining bathroom housed a tub of matching proportions to the rest of the environment and, as I turned the huge tap, the clankings and gurglings that heralded the eventual approach of the warm water were all very late night horror film.

I took a bath and prepared myself for bed. But before I retired and put out the light, I mentally drew a circle of light which I extended from my bed well out into the room. Then, from within, I addressed those I knew to be present rather along these lines: 'Now, all of you, I know you are there and, fair enough, this is your domain and I am the guest; so kindly afford me the privileges of a guest, a quiet and undisturbed night; no phenomena, I don't wish to see any of you in physical form as I am perfectly capable of seeing you with my psychic eye if I wish; so with all courtesy and due deference to your rank and dignity I bid you goodnight.' With that I raised the atmosphere within my circle to a level which would inhibit phenomena and enjoyed a perfect night's sleep.

I can hear somebody asking, 'What does she mean when she says she raised the atmosphere to a level?' and so on. What I mean is this: there is a comfortable level of vibration or frequency for everything. Matter manifests at one frequency, phenomena of a psychic nature manifests at another, pure thought at another. Or, if you want to be scientific about it, let us come back to our X-rays and gamma rays. You can't see them, but they can be generated by a machine and that machine can be turned off so that they cannot manifest unless their particular energy frequency is generated. And so it is with psychic phenomena. By the use of the trained mind, or trained thinking processes, one can build up an atmosphere that encourages physical manifestations, or generate a mental energy that inhibits it. Doubting Thomases or disbelievers often unconsciously generate the latter.

I have experienced sitting with certain selected people who can take a psychic 'high' with comfort. One can generate a high psychic or occult vibration mentally, but again I am worried about the terminology because it isn't really 'high' or 'low', but 'fast' and 'slow'. The faster the vibes the more difficult for the sitters to cope and the more difficult for anything wishing to materialize to do so. In fact, I have watched a psychic 'high' produce headaches, disorientation and the type of side effects normally associated with exposure to radiation or X-rays. This applies particularly to dealings with the elemental kingdoms; not everyone can cope with fire elementals or salamanders, for example.

In ritual magic I have witnessed students experiencing

great difficulty with one or other element. One lady I knew could not cope with the sylphs, a problem she shared with the late Dion Fortune, incidentally. Each time she invoked them, candles would blow out, curtains breeze apart, electric lights start swaying, and so on. Someone else I knew couldn't make it with the salamanders and had a series of blown fuses, burned food and the like. Yet another friend of mine suffers from watery problems so, you see, everyone is not suited to every aspect of magic and we return to our analogy of looking for a gas leak with a lighted match. The occult is a great exposer of weaknesses, and we all have them somewhere or other in our personalities or we wouldn't need to be here on earth to learn.

To raise an atmosphere sufficiently high or fast to inhibit phenomena one can either employ pure mind power (which I find the most effective) or use a ritual designed to keep everything out of a given area for a set period of time.

Dismissals

One of the mistakes most commonly made by the beginner in the magical or occult field is to invoke a force or energy and fail to place it. Some people find it fun simply to sit together and act as a sort of group generating station. 'Gosh, what a lovely power we've made!' they exclaim, and then promptly chat about the affairs of the day over tea and cakes. But what happens to the force generated? IT HAS TO GO SOMEWHERE. If one commands, invokes or evokes a cosmic energy, archetypal force, discarnate entity or external intelligence, one needs to either place it or dismiss it.

Spirits of the elements invoked during ritual magic should be appropriately dismissed to the points of the compass, to return to their group element WITH THANKS AND LOVE. They should never be simply left around. Energies invoked and unused, as I have explained before, will attach themselves to whoever is the most psychic person around, or whoever they feel an affinity with, and that could mean sleepless nights, nightmares, headaches, unaccountable sickness, and so on.

So, if you ask a sylph, salamander, gnome or ondine to help you, DO PLEASE SAY 'THANK YOU' and ask it to return to its own kind in the spirit of love. It's as simple as that. And, if you notice a heavy build-up of psychic atmosphere when you are seated with a group of like-minded people, for goodness' sake use it for the good of something or somebody. There is bound to be some sick person you know, or someone with a nagging problem who could do with a boost right then.

Have you ever noticed how it is when several people sit together round a fire with the lights low and start to talk about spooky things? Somehow the atmosphere gathers momentum and a familiar sound like the gurgle in a water pipe takes on sinister undertones and causes everyone to jump. What happens is that the combined thought force of those present, all centred on phenomena, actually produces a fertile breeding ground for its manifestation, and that's when the cups are likely to jump off the shelf or the spirit of deceased Uncle Joe start rapping. In other words, it's all in the mind!

Vacuums
Nature abhors a vacuum, say the scientists, and this is equally applicable to matters occult or magical. If you ever have recourse to exorcism as a means of clearing unwanted vibes from a room or removing a link from an individual, for goodness' sake DO NOT LEAVE A VACUUM. Fill it with something more appropriate to the person or environment concerned. For example, if you are asked to clear the atmosphere in a home where there are several young children and where the parents, although not necessarily religious in any practising way, are Christian oriented, once you have swept the place clear of the unwanted vibes, invoke a ray that would be harmonious to the family, such as the Virgin Mary in a Catholic home or simply the Christ cross.

Don't try calling in anything stimulating, especially if there are teenagers around, and remember that, for the average westerner, some eastern vibes tend to create mystical thought patterns that are fine for meditation but are not always helpful in everyday practical life. The best thing to do is to spend some time talking to the occupants to see what would be best for them. If they are sad and depressed, a cheerful atmosphere would best benefit them, whereas with people who are hyperactive, nervous or over-tense, a more soothing and calming ray would be better. If you are unsure of your rays, use colours, as a colour automatically evokes the archetypal force with which it is associated.

Blues and greens are soothing and in keeping with the Egyptian goddesses Isis and Nephthys. The nature kingdoms in Pantheism respond to the greens and browns of earth, whereas the stimulatory reds and purples belong to Geburah and Chesed in the Qabalistic tradition, or Ares and Zeus in the Greek. Golds and oranges relate to the sun gods in all systems and are always healthful and energizing. But, whatever you do, NEVER SIMPLY CLEAR AN ATMOSPHERE AND LEAVE NOTHING IN ITS PLACE. SET A NEW ONE THAT IS RIGHT FOR THOSE WHO WILL USE THE PLACE, in so far as you are able to judge it to be correct.

The scriptures will tell you the dangers of removing an evil spirit or leaving the door open for 'seven more to enter', and this vacuum principle applies just as strongly in the psychology of everyday life. My wise old nanny used to say, 'the devil finds work for idle hands', the same thing said in a different context.

CHAPTER TWELVE

EXORCISMS

This is NOT a textbook on magical practices and procedures, so my advice must be: don't attempt exorcisms, either of places or people, unless you are trained to a standard where you know what you are doing and are not likely to cause the sufferers worse problems than they already have. There have been many cases reported in the national press of people suffering from mental illness who have been taken to exorcists, only to end up by taking their own life plus that of a few other people *en route*. Not every case of mental illness is a possession, as I have already illustrated. The poor soul who has a slight deformity in his brain may state emphatically that he sees demons but this will simply be the malfunctioning of his reasoning faculties.

Occult healing is a highly specialized field and, unless you are skilled in diagnosing *outside* the aura, i.e. able to scan the surrounding ether to see if there is something lurking around which has no business there, leave well alone. Better to let the medical profession handle it, as they are sometimes able to help the sufferers to eject it for themselves, the best way in the long run. Good religious intent or faith in this or that creed does not necessarily endow one with the powers of exorcism, as many an ordained clergyman has found to his chagrin. There are true stories I could tell to illustrate this, but these would make a book in themselves!

If you know what you are doing, however, the 'caller/coverer' system is the safest for exorcism; just be sure that whatever is removed is despatched safely and with love to where it belongs and not left wandering around to make a nuisance of itself to the next person passing with an open aura.. Would-be exorcists should ensure that they know how to avoid picking up what they have withdrawn from the possessed person. During my years in occultism I have encountered endless cases of dabblers who have managed to dislodge a possessing entity, only to find themselves landed with it, much to their dismay! Not a pleasant experience, I can assure you.

The student occultist is more likely to encounter links or auric limpets, especially if working in the field of occult healing. The former can be picked up in several ways: by an over-possessive relationship with some other living person, by the influence of someone who has passed on, or simply by strong thought patterns from others trying to enforce their will in some way. These can be easily severed with the use of a clearing ray if one is working direct from the mind, or by ritualistic means if one is into ceremonial magic. But again may I caution the healer to be sure that both points of severance are sealed and healed. In other words, seal the aura of the patient at the place where the link has been cut, and then return the link to whoever has sent it out originally and seal it back into the sender's aura; if you are a well-trained psychic you will have no difficulty in visualizing the sender and closing him up safely and soundly. If you are not able to do this, then you shouldn't be attempting this kind of work in the first place.

Auric limpets are very common and represent the loose floating dust and debris of the lower astral. Often people complain of some discomfort where no physical cause can be found. Some piece of astral 'gunge' has probably attached itself to them; perhaps in a crowded room or public place, or through brushing against some unscrupulous person who is psychically 'unclean'. Often people have said to me, 'I've never felt quite right since I had tea with so and so.' This is usually an indication that some unpleasant or incompatible energies have passed between the persons concerned and there is a need for an auric cleansing. The best colours for cleaning up an aura are blue and white and, again, due deference should be paid to beliefs adhered to by the patient.

Links, limpets or energies, or force fields of any kind alien to the environment they are in, should be RETURNED TO THEIR RIGHTFUL SPHERE OF ACTIVITY or, as I prefer to call it, TIME ZONE. Very often one encounters spirits or intelligences that have accidentally strayed and become 'lost'. There is nothing deliberately offensive about them but they are frequently on the defensive, as you might well be if you found yourself in some strange place where you didn't know a soul or understand the tongue! The language of occult procedure is universal in that it can be conveyed by thought. So send your thoughts to whatever or whoever is lost and re-direct them to their own path. And if you do not know what I am talking about I suggest you either leave well alone or start at the beginning, if you are an earnest seeker, and learn your art in a stable and disciplined fashion.

Amulets and Talismans

One is frequently asked how efficacious amulets and talismans are, especially for psychic self-defence. Sorry to come back to the same old theme again, but it really does rest with what you believe they can do for you. A correctly cast magical talisman carries with it the influence of the ray or rays infused into it by the magician who has cast it.

A dear friend of mine sent me a correctly assembled talisman of Venus as a present. The instructions which went with it were for the owner to concentrate upon it at least once a day and FIRMLY BELIEVE that it would work. There are, therefore, several factors involved here. First of all, the faith of the owner or wearer; secondly, the power of the magician who has effected the casting; and, thirdly, the collective power of the system or tradition in which it has been cast.

Sometimes one does not *consciously* subscribe to a belief in such charms, but the subconscious will accept them. In such cases the owners tend to dismiss them as amusing presents and yet not seem surprised when they actually work. The converse may apply and I have known sincere believers, or so they say, who have received no benefit at all. Weigh each aspect one against another and decide for yourself, dear reader.

CHAPTER THIRTEEN

DIET AND PSYCHIC DEVELOPMENT

Many share the view that a vegetarian regime or some other specially designed diet is an aid to psychic or spiritual development and also serves to keep away the 'nasties'. Is there any truth in this?

A very light diet, such as veganism, refines the body to a degree and can help open up the mind to other dimensions of awareness. But, as I once heard an eminent vegetarian say at a London lecture, over-sensitiveness can sometimes prove a problem in everyday life. So, while it may suit many to espouse some refining dietary cause, it is not necessarily a protective measure, as an over-sensitive aura can prove just as much an occult problem as a totally insensitive one.

Besides, it is a mistake to imagine that because a person abstains from certain foods he is more gifted psychically or more spiritually advanced than the next man. One of the best psychics I know is a meat eater, but equally I have vegetarian friends who are excellent sensitives, so judgments should never be made on this issue alone.

Food tastes are often tempered by environment and those raised on one type of diet sometimes find it physically difficult to switch round later in life, no matter how lofty their ideals and ethics.

It is also well to remember that all living things contain a spirit or life force and sometimes a greater degree of consciousness than we give them credit for, and a lettuce is as much a part of the Creator as a hen or a cow. So no spiritual smugness should be entertained, but it is as well to note that the human body (and therefore the mind) does function better when fed in a balanced fashion, in keeping with the design of its internal organs. Also, all human beings are unique unto themselves and, as any radionics expert will tell you, foods that suit some can cause illness in others.

The master with whom I learned used to caution us, 'No red meat, alcohol or sexual activity for at least three hours prior to a working.' This is purely practical advice, if you care to look into it, mainly concerned with the conservation of vital energies and alert mental faculties necessary to the efficiency of the working. I have always found it to be wise counsel, but in the ultimate analysis it is a question of knowing the chemical balance and requirements of your own body on the one hand, and the dictates of your true conscience on the other.

CHAPTER FOURTEEN

ANIMALS AND PSYCHIC SELF-DEFENCE

We now come to the role of animals in psychic self-defence, for they can and do have one. Some animals are more skilled at warding off evil than many people who fancy themselves to be greater, wiser and more evolved than they really are. I once had an ordinary black-and-white cat which was perfectly capable of guarding a medium in trance and only a high initiate could have broken through his defence. Too much nonsense is talked about the place of the animal kingdoms in the evolutionary scheme of things; fortunately the master with whom I trained put me straight on a few points in this direction quite early on in my studies. Which brings me to a true story.

Some twenty-five years ago, myself and four others were sitting with a trance medium when the guide invited questions. One of those present, a very young lady with an exalted opinion of her spiritual potential, was quick off the mark. 'Yes, sir, I have a question,' she chipped in. 'Will you say which of us in this room is the most advanced soul?' I can recall feeling terribly embarrassed and wishing the floor would open up and hide me, when the guide answered, 'Yes, I'd be happy to.' There was an awkward pause before he continued, 'In the chair in the corner of this room there is a little black-and-white cat asleep; its spirit is out of its body and with me. That is the most advanced soul in this room. . . .' I have often thought back on that statement and not without a tear, perhaps of humility and perhaps of gratitude, for being privileged to work with so wise a guide.

From the aforesaid you, my reader, will have gathered that I do not subscribe to those schools of thought which teach that our souls were formerly in animal bodies, and so on, but rather to the belief that each evolutionary stream or impulse is separate unto itself; and that there are planets, perhaps in some far distant galaxy, where people are the pets and the animals have advanced mentally to become the reasoning and dominating species.

Yes, there are animals which are capable of sincere and reliable psychic defence, but there again they are very much like people in that some are better at it than others. As with ourselves, it all depends on where they learned their art: in the temples of Egypt or Tibet, or in the judgment halls of Atlantis, or even in some tribe of advanced animal-type people in another corner of the universe. . . .

CHAPTER FIFTEEN

DOS AND DON'TS

Many sincere folk envisage the Aquarian Age as one where every man is his own or her own occultist, but in view of what I have written, there will be those who have their doubts. Much as I would love to say that this is a field in which anyone interested should 'have a go' I cannot, as yet, in conscience do so. Probably because, during my years in healing, I encountered too many psychic casualties. But I do have faith in the future and that faith extends to the hope that, once this planet has been purged of its negative vibes, its denizens will have a purer link with the cosmos outside its own immediate environment. Of course this will set up another, entirely different, set of problems but, as I see it, mankind will have a clearer view of other dimensions and therefore be better aware of who and what it is he is up against.

A certain strength of mind, stability or integration of personality is necessary for occult work proper, but there are many psychics who do not probe too deeply into matters hidden and, therefore, are not likely to encounter the dangers of the faster byways of metaphysical experience, so for them the requirements are not so stringent. I will list a few dos and don'ts that I feel might be of help to those who really feel drawn to psychism, occultism or mysticism.

Beware of those so-termed 'friendly' entities who supposedly wake you up at 3 am to dictate the secrets of the universe! I once knew a woman who was a physical wreck because of sleepless nights caused, she informed me, by a 'great and wise guide' who insisted upon having her perform his bidding at some ungodly hour. No great wise being, this! Quite the reverse. Any purported entity who is so insensitive as to be unaware of the normal needs of the human body is hardly from exalted realms. I know that if any such being disturbed my sleep, it would quickly be sent on its way with a flea in its etheric ear.

I am perfectly aware that there are spiritual helpers who tactfully direct those with whom they are destined to work — to this town, that walk of life, this partner or that source of power. But, when a gentle helping hand becomes an order, there is something VERY wrong.

Into this category I also place those psychic show-offs who jump up at other people's public meetings (or private circles) and effect a take-over. Folks, if you want a platform, go race a car, jump on a soap box at Hyde Park Corner, or join the local amateur dramatic society, but DON'T PLEASE inflict your ego trip on the poor, long-suffering public under the guise of a communicating spook! Or it may even be the spook who is ego tripping! I've met them all in my time.

Next point: nobody *owns* anybody or anything else in the universe. Voluntary associations or partnerships can be formed, but I recall an occasion in the south of England when a renowned medium went into trance: the guide announced himself and was greeted with an angry shout from the audience to the effect of 'what are you doing through her? you're supposed to be working with my group. . . .' Absolutely true!

Don't condemn the occult folk down the street because they do not exactly follow what you believe to be the truth. In fact, never condemn or judge ANYBODY, it's totally unethical to do so. If you really disapprove of the way they live their lives, try sending them kind thoughts; after all, you might learn from the spiritual exchange. But at the same time, don't follow any and every psychic fad in an effort to be frightfully liberal. That is just as dangerous. Select what you feel to be the right path for you, examine its ethics and live by it to the best of your conscience, always keeping your mind open enough to adjust your views if evidence proves you to have made a mistake. Science isn't always the bogey to run from when it comes up with a few 'facts', but science itself is also changing so rapidly that one of its respected fellows was recently heard to remark on television that higher mathematics had become 'more esoteric than a guru'! So sometimes the psychic or occultist is a jump ahead.

If you are of a rigid religious persuasion resist the temptation to condemn all other systems and traditions as 'black'. It is interesting to note that in mass hypnotic experiments involving students from many countries and many creeds, when regressed to a state of pre-birth they all agreed they were not bound by any particular earth religion. Only the ensuing environment seems to leave its mark on the later moral judgments of the psyche, but once liberated from the body, the spirit returns to a state of cosmic consciousness which is not *necessarily* tainted by earthly interpretations of universal principles.

I once heard a well-known guide, who claimed Red Indian connections, exclaim when questioned from the audience, 'I am a Red Man because you like to hear Red Men, but I could be anything you wanted from any period of history, it matters not as long as I get my message to you.' A dear little elderly medium I once knew used to bring through the spirit of a fundamentalist preacher who had obviously carried *his* hell, fire and brimstone philosophy over with him. I recall asking him why he still followed that way of thinking after he had seen a wider view in outer time. He replied, 'She fashions me into this mould; if I were to tell her what I *really* know her mind couldn't take it and I'd lose one of my many channels. Besides, it helps her, poor soul!' I hope this serves to illustrate my point.

For those involving themselves in ceremonial magic, in addition to my former advice regarding not mixing systems, I would also advise you to keep to the correct colours, invocations, robes, planetary hours, and so on, for the tradition you decide upon, and refrain from injecting some different emphasis simply because you like the feel of it. Wiser folk than you, who have gone before, have usually tried and tested these details, so they are incorporated with good reason.

There can be danger in allowing persons outside the group or lodge to handle magical instruments, and these should always be kept in a clean and safe place and regularly checked over. Some magicians re-dedicate their impedimenta prior to each working, which is not really necessary, although if it puts their mind at rest then so much the better, particularly if a piece hasn't been used for some time.

Magical instruments should only have associations with the person or persons handling them in an occult capacity; cross vibes on any piece can be a source of trouble, especially where the invocation of the elements is concerned. I knew a gentleman who acquired a sword that had been consecrated for ceremonial magic and which had never been cleared after the user had died suddenly. He hung it on his wall as an ornament; and then things started to happen. As many occultists will know, the sword commands the sylphs to the east, so that the phenomena this gentleman's family experienced were all associated with uncanny draughts, objects being moved to face east, window catches falling off for no logical reason, and so forth. Fortunately somebody put him in touch with me and I was able to clear the piece and allow the sylphs to return to their own domains. If you are a collector it does NOT do to add former items from the regalia or impedimenta of a magician to your collection. ANYTHING might happen.

If you have been working with a lodge and wish to leave, take your personal items with you and either burn them or clear them. Use the correct colours, instruments and accoutrements for the tradition or system in which you have decided to work and, if you are unsure as to what to follow, why not simply design your own rituals as suggested by William Gray in his excellent book *Magical Ritual Methods*. As long as you stay with one thing at a time you will be safe but, until you are quite sure as to what mixes and what does not, keep securely anchored to the tried and tested.

There are certain useful little occult practices cropping up in this or that system which are often discussed in articles and magazines. These include such things as the Scales of Maat in the Egyptian system, which is used in cases where one is unsure about someone's intentions; and the Net of Hephaestus, which is a 'holding' ray in the Greek system. These may all sound very clever when expounded by 'old hands' or intellectualized by fireside occultists with a good sense of journalism, but it is not wise to experiment with them outside the context of the system from which they claim their source of power.

As ritualistic practices vary in each tradition, it would not be possible for me to enumerate any one set of disciplines, but the sincere student who is destined to succeed will be led to the correct reference books or tutor and, if you find you are not getting anywhere, do remember that like attracts like, so perhaps you are searching along the wrong alleyway.

The Ethics
There is no absolute truth, except at the centre point; therefore, in our present stage of development, truth for each person is whatever causes them to relate to the ethics of cosmic law at any given period in their evolutionary cycle. What may seem ethical to a young soul may not to an older or more time-travelled spirit. And so, you may justly ask, what guidelines are there for those who wish to pursue the path, be it via mysticism, psychism or occultism?

Love, self-honesty, selflessness, understanding, caring, all these are virtues to aim for, inasmuch as each individual is able to realize them. So also are strength of purpose, loyalty and firmness. Recognize the enemies of light by their hatred, self-esteem, self-centredness, lack of understanding and caring or, alternatively, their lack of purpose, disloyalty and vacillation. The old or time-travelled soul has sensitivity, acknowledges all other life forms and is able to look outward into the universe. Sorry, folks, I don't go along with all this introversion stuff and seeking within; one finds oneself and overcomes one's own problems through relating to the problems of others, just as the teacher learns more from his pupils than he did from his textbooks.

The old soul will see the life force in a plant, animal or breeze. The young soul is too tied up in himself to be aware of such subtleties. The old soul can sit in silence and harmony is his nectar. The young soul thrives on noise and disharmony and is usually frightened of silence because it exposes him to himself. All these are pointers for the would-be seeker of the path.

Although in this book I have discussed various methods of healing which are or can be carried out by trained personnel, it is my own personal belief that, as we progress into the Aquarian Age, every man will be his own healer, for self-healing is the thing of the future. But even the principles of self-healing need to be learned and understood before they can be effectively applied, and nowhere is discipline and honesty more essential than when coming to personal terms with the 'self'; so a good groundwork in cosmic law and its general functions provides a secure framework from which to venture forth into the individualization of the 'new age'. Once man has mastered the art of self-healing, he will be able to step confidently into the metaphysical universe without the need for priests, occultists, mediums or intermediaries of any kind, because he will have direct personal communication with his true cosmic family.

We of humanity tend to walk the tight-rope of reason across the abyss of ignorance, in our never-ending quest for knowledge and our pressing desire to penetrate to even greater depths in the uncharted territories of human consciousness. The only reliable guide we have is the light of true love; I do not mean what is popularly passed off as that emotion, but rather the deep, unselfish universal love that is a constant beacon for our guidance at ALL LEVELS THROUGHOUT INFINITY. As like attracts like, if you follow this principle you won't go far wrong.

INDEX